The Great Reversal

www.worldbank.org/en/research

The Great Reversal

Prospects, Risks, and Policies
in International Development
Association (IDA) Countries

Tommy Chrimes, Bram Gootjes,
M. Ayhan Kose, and Collette Wheeler

... acceleration of economic development which will promote higher standards of living and economic and social progress in the less-developed countries is desirable not only in the interests of those countries but also in the interests of the international community as a whole ...

International Development Association
Articles of Agreement
September 24, 1960

At its founding, the International Development Association was charged with a simple yet noble mission—to raise standards of living and build momentum for growth in developing countries. But the landscape we face today is far more complex: declining progress in our fight against poverty, an existential climate crisis, food insecurity, fragility, a fledgling pandemic recovery, and conflict that touches lives beyond the frontlines ...

Ajay Banga
World Bank Group President
Remarks at the IDA Midterm Review
December 6, 2023

Contents

Tables

Acknowledgments

This study is a publication of the Prospects Group and was produced under the general guidance of Indermit Gill. His feedback and constant support helped deepen the analysis presented here.

The publication has been possible only because of many brilliant colleagues. Lorëz Qehaja has provided exceptional and indefatigable research assistance, conducting data work and statistical analysis along with the impressive Shijie Shi and Vasiliki Papagianni. Excellent research support was also provided by Mattia Coppo, Franco Diaz Laura, Maria Hazel Macadangdang, Rafaela Martinho Henriques, Urja Singh Thapa, Kaltrina Temaj, and Matias Urzua.

Feedback from various experts has helped shape and enhance our work. This has included insightful views from Masood Ahmed, Timothy Callen, Delfin Go, Sanjeev Gupta, Graham Hacche, Edith Kikoni, Timothy Lane, Akihiko Nishio, James Rowe, Raju Singh, and Rudi Steinbach. Their perspectives and wisdom have been invaluable.

We also received helpful reviews and specific inputs from Joseph Mawejje, Kate McKinnon, Valerie Mercer-Blackman, and Kersten Stamm, as well as key thematic contributions from John Baffes, Samuel Hill, Dominik Peschel, Naotaka Sugawara, and Hamza Zahid. Reina Kawai, Dohan Kim, Jiwon Lee, and Takuma Tanaka provided incisive additional reviews. We are thankful to our colleagues in the Prospects Group who provided thoughtful early feedback at an internal seminar.

We are grateful to Joseph Rebello for his considered suggestions throughout the process, and to him, Nandita Roy, Kristen Milhollin, and Mariana Lozzi Teixeira for managing media relations and social media outreach. We thank Graeme Littler for editorial and web support. We owe a particular debt of gratitude to Adriana Maximiliano for her outstanding work coordinating the print publication, in collaboration with Jason Barrett and Onyekachi Wosu.

About the Authors

Tommy Chrimes is a Senior Economist in the World Bank Group's Prospects Group. Previously, he served as an Advisor to the UK Executive Directors at the International Monetary Fund and World Bank Group. Before that, he worked for the UK civil service in various international economics and policy roles.

Bram Gootjes is an Economist in the World Bank Group's Prospects Group. Previously, he worked as a Researcher in the Department of Global Economics and Management at the University of Groningen in the Netherlands.

M. Ayhan Kose is Deputy Chief Economist of the World Bank Group and Director of the World Bank Group's Prospects Group. He previously worked in the Research and Western Hemisphere Departments of the International Monetary Fund. He is a Nonresident Senior Fellow at the Brookings Institution, a Research Fellow at the Centre for Economic Policy Research, a Dean's Fellow at the University of Virginia's Darden School of Business, and a Research Associate at the Center for Applied Macroeconomic Analysis.

Collette Wheeler is a Senior Economist in the World Bank Group's Prospects Group. Previously, she worked in the World Bank Group's Macroeconomics, Trade, and Investment Global Practice for the Europe and Central Asia Region. Prior to that, she worked in economic consulting.

Abbreviations

EMDEs   emerging market and developing economies
FCS   fragile and conflict-affected situations
FDI   foreign direct investment
GDP   gross domestic product
IBRD   International Bank for Reconstruction and Development
IDA   International Development Association
LIC   low-income country
OECD   Organisation for Economic Co-operation and Development

OVERVIEW

For the world's most vulnerable countries, the outlook is bleak.

The World Bank Group's International Development Association (IDA) provides support to the poorest and most vulnerable countries in the world—support that has real impact. The 75 economies currently eligible for grants and low-interest loans from IDA account for just under one-quarter of the global population but more than 70 percent of the world's extreme poor and only 3 percent of global output. They faced significant challenges long before the COVID-19 pandemic. Yet they had made notable progress on several key development indicators in the last few decades: on access to basic services, life expectancy, and poverty reduction, for example. Their debt vulnerabilities, however, continued to increase, along with structural concerns. These persistent challenges are holding back progress and threatening to erode it. Significant gaps between IDA countries and the rest of the world remain across a broad range of development metrics.

Amid overlapping crises, IDA countries face their weakest recovery in decades.

The overlapping crises of 2020-23 have compounded the development challenges confronting IDA countries. The emergence of COVID-19 saw GDP growth in these countries fall to 0.3 percent in 2020: the lowest rate recorded since the early 1980s. The weakness was broad-based, but small states experienced particularly sharp contractions.

Other shocks, including conflicts, a sharp increase in global inflation, a rapid rise in interest rates, and a tightening in global financial conditions, have undermined the recovery since 2020. Sovereign spreads for IDA countries have increased markedly relative to those in other emerging market and developing economies (EMDEs). External financial flows to these countries also fell in 2022. In the near term, growth in IDA countries is expected to remain subdued, with 2020-24 set to be the weakest half decade of growth since the early 1990s (figure O.1). The combination of prepandemic vulnerabilities, recent overlapping crises in the first part of this decade, and wider problems—including the effects of climate change and increases in violence and conflict—is weighing heavily on these countries' economic and social development.

A historic reversal in development is under way.

Amid stunted economic recoveries, one in three IDA countries is poorer now than on the eve of the pandemic. Over the five years from 2020 to 2024, half of IDA countries are set to experience a widening gap in their per capita incomes with respect to those of advanced economies. The pandemic has undone three years of progress, and other crises have taken a heavy toll on poverty reduction. In 2023, the share of people living in extreme poverty in these countries is estimated to have been more than eight times that in the rest of the world. These countries account for 92 percent of the world's food-insecure people, after a doubling of their food-insecure populations since 2019. Half of IDA countries are currently in debt distress or at high risk of it.

Stagnation could become more entrenched, with a danger of deeper reversals.

The key risk is that the current weak economic trajectory for IDA countries persists or deteriorates, leading to a lost decade in development. IDA countries are particularly exposed to climate-change-related natural disasters, which have become more common and costlier over time. Instances of violence and conflict have also increased sharply in many IDA countries in the 2020s; they pose a further threat to economic stability and growth.

Global headwinds make progress harder to achieve.

Any weakening in long-term global growth prospects would likely weigh heavily on the already-subdued outlook for IDA countries. An escalation in geopolitical tensions, fragmentation of trade and investment networks, weaker-than-expected near-term growth in major economies, or any combination of these factors could impede growth in IDA countries. A protracted period of tighter financial conditions would worsen fiscal and external imbalances. Dependence on a narrow range of exports, limited fiscal space, and constrained access to financial markets leave IDA countries particularly exposed to external shocks.

IDA countries have high economic potential that can *be unlocked.*

History offers many examples of IDA countries that have overcome multifaceted development challenges. Large economies such as China, India, and the Republic of Korea successfully graduated from IDA eligibility (that is, they once were eligible for IDA resources, but their economies have grown sufficiently that they no longer meet the eligibility criteria) and are now important engines of the global economy. Current IDA countries have important attributes that can be harnessed to help generate future growth and development. Many of them possess abundant natural resources, including substantial reserves of minerals

FIGURE O.1 **IDA countries: Prospects, risks, and policies**

IDA countries are set to experience, in 2020-24, their weakest half decade of growth since the early 1990s, halting their catch-up in per capita incomes relative to those in advanced economies in more than half of them. Progress in reducing extreme poverty in these countries has also stalled, and food insecurity has surged. IDA countries have the potential to reap large demographic dividends. To do so, however, they need to implement comprehensive policy packages to accelerate growth and meet large investment needs.

A. Annual average GDP growth

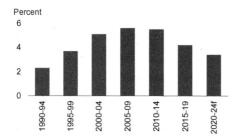

B. Share with lower growth in GDP per capita than that of advanced economies

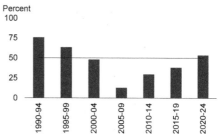

C. Share of population in extreme poverty, 1990-2030

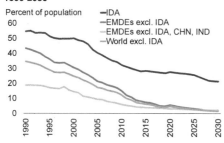

D. Food insecurity

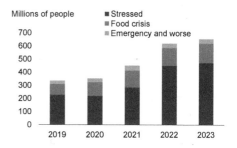

E. Working-age population

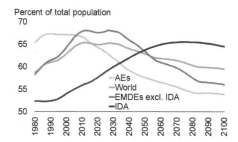

F. Annual investment needs for a resilient and low-carbon pathway, 2022-30

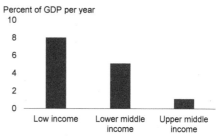

Sources: GRFC (database); Mahler and Lakner (2022); WDI database; World Bank (2022, 2024); World Population Prospects database; World Bank, Poverty and Inequality Platform; World Bank.
Note: AEs= advanced economies; CHN = China; e = estimate; EMDEs = emerging market and developing economies; excl. = excluding; f = forecast; GDP = gross domestic product; IDA = IDA countries; IND = India.
B. GDP per capita aggregates are calculated as aggregated GDP divided by aggregate population. GDP aggregates are calculated using real U.S. dollar GDP weights at average 2010-19 prices and market exchange rates.
C. Sample includes up to 75 IDA-eligible countries and 83 EMDEs excluding IDA countries. "World" includes 158 countries. Poverty data are from Mahler and Lakner (2022) and the World Bank Poverty and Inequality Platform.
D. Sample includes data for up to 50 IDA countries.
E. Population-weighted averages. Working-age population is defined as those ages 15 to 64 years. Population projections come from the UN World Population Prospects database.
F. Bars show estimates of the annual investment needs to build countries' resilience to climate change and put them on track to reduce emissions by 70 percent by 2050. Depending on data availability, estimates include investment needs related to transport, energy, water, urban adaptations, industry, and landscape.

critical to the global energy transition. Many also have the potential to reap large demographic dividends, with working-age populations expected to surge over the next half century.

These resource and demographic endowments carry well-documented risks but, if well-managed, represent major opportunities. Various countries that have graduated from IDA eligibility made significant progress on policy reform packages and accelerated their development paths. If the current cohort of IDA countries can implement similarly comprehensive policy reforms with the necessary financial and technical support of the global community, they will be primed to better deploy their natural and human resources and make decisive progress in delivering strong, sustainable, and inclusive growth.

Ambitious national policies are needed to accelerate investment growth.

IDA countries need substantial investment to meet their development goals, including investment for climate adaptation, human capital development, and digital transformation. Creating the conditions to accelerate investment growth hinges on the implementation of comprehensive policy packages. Policy makers in IDA countries need to restore fiscal sustainability and strengthen policy and institutional frameworks. This could also promote more effective management of natural resources.

At the same time, these countries should seek to improve education and health outcomes and dismantle barriers that hamper women, youth, and other disadvantaged groups from obtaining productive jobs, thus leveraging demographic dividends. In addition, they should undertake measures to enhance resilience, address climate-related risks, and better integrate themselves into the global economy. By doing so, IDA countries can significantly increase the likelihood of stronger and sustained investment growth. This can in turn be a catalyst for promoting income growth, accelerating poverty reduction, and bridging infrastructure gaps.

Global support is essential to restart progress in development.

Significant financial support from the global community is essential to enable progress in IDA countries and overcome the serious risk of more protracted stagnation. Enhanced cooperation on global policy issues—including fighting climate change, facilitating more timely and effective debt restructuring, and supporting cross-border trade and investment—is also essential to help support IDA countries' efforts and avert a lost decade in development. History makes it clear that closing income and development gaps between the poorest and wealthiest nations benefits *all* economies.

References

GRFC (Global Report on Food Crises) Database 2016-2024 (accessed February 4, 2024). https://www.fsinplatform.org/our-data.

Mahler, D. G., and C. Lakner. 2022. "The Impact of COVID-19 on Global Inequality and Poverty." Policy Research Working Paper 10198, World Bank, Washington, DC.

WDI (World Development Indicators) database (accessed March 29, 2024). https:// datatopics.worldbank.org/world-development-indicators/.

World Bank. 2022. "Climate and Development: An Agenda for Action." Emerging Insights from World Bank Group 2021-22 Country Climate Development Reports, World Bank, Washington, DC.

World Bank. 2024. "The Magic of Investment Accelerations." In *Global Economic Prospects*, January. Washington, DC: World Bank.

World Population Prospects database (accessed March 2, 2024). https:// population. un.org/wpp/.

The outlook for the countries eligible for IDA resources is bleak. As a group, they are experiencing their weakest recovery in decades amid overlapping crises, leading to a historic setback in development. The stagnation implied by this weak recovery and setback could become more deeply entrenched, with a risk of further reversals as global headwinds make progress even more difficult. Despite these challenges, these countries possess significant economic potential that can be harnessed with ambitious national policies to spur investment and growth. Support from the global community is crucial to reignite progress in development.

Background

The global crises since 2020 have hit the 75 countries eligible for grants and low-interest loans from the World Bank Group's IDA hard.[1] Development is reversing in a major way in these countries, which are among the poorest and most vulnerable in the world. As a group, they are struggling through their weakest half decade of growth since the early 1990s. A third of the countries eligible for IDA resources (hereafter, "IDA countries") are projected to have lower per capita incomes in 2024 than in 2019. Amid stunted recoveries, more than half have seen income gaps widen relative to those in advanced economies since the pandemic. Progress on poverty reduction has stalled, and food insecurity has surged. Many IDA countries are in debt distress. Most are also particularly exposed to the growing impacts of climate change. Fiscal positions are strained, and investment needs are rising.

IDA countries were already facing a raft of development challenges before the succession of crises of 2020-23. But these crises, including the COVID-19 outbreak, multiple conflicts, a sharp increase in global inflation, elevated interest rates, and tighter global financial conditions, have compounded the challenges, putting key development objectives further out of reach and leaving IDA countries particularly vulnerable to new shocks.

Yet progress is still possible—not least because IDA countries have significant untapped economic potential. Many of these countries have rich stores of natural

---

[1] The IDA, founded in 1960, aims to reduce poverty by providing grants, as well as loans at zero or low interest rates, to the world's most vulnerable countries for programs that boost economic growth, reduce inequalities, and improve people's living conditions.

resources and favorable demographics; leveraging these advantages effectively, however, will require careful and concerted effort. Implementing ambitious policy packages has the potential to make a significant difference, supporting investment accelerations to underpin growth, as has happened in many countries in the past. The challenge for national policy makers is to pursue policies that can capitalize on these countries' economic advantages to drive strong and sustainable growth. In doing so, they will also need the support of the global community.

Against this background, this study addresses the following questions:

- What are the key economic features of IDA countries?

- How have the overlapping global crises of 2020-23 affected these countries?

- What are the near-term economic prospects and risks for IDA countries?

- What key national policy interventions can promote growth and advance development objectives in these countries?

- How can the global community best support IDA countries?

Contributions

This study approaches the 75 IDA countries as a group, while acknowledging the considerable economic diversity among them. It makes five unique contributions. First, it considers the key features of IDA countries in the context of macroeconomic developments in the years up to 2020. Second, it presents the first comprehensive review of developments since the COVID-19 pandemic and subsequent crises, documenting how these crises have added to the challenges facing IDA countries. It highlights the significant output losses these countries have suffered, as well as their lack of progress in poverty reduction and in the convergence of their per capita incomes with those in advanced economies. Third, it assesses near-term prospects for these countries and examines the important risks they face. Fourth, it considers several factors that could potentially play in their favor. Finally, it outlines the national and global policy interventions needed to help IDA countries tackle the challenges confronting them and capitalize on their comparative advantages.

Main findings

Key features. Most IDA countries have low per capita income levels: this is a primary determinant of eligibility for IDA assistance (which requires per capita incomes less than $1,315 in fiscal year 2024). The IDA also supports some countries with per capita incomes above this threshold that lack the creditworthiness needed to borrow from the International Bank for Reconstruction and Development (IBRD), the IDA's sister institution serving middle-income and creditworthy low-income countries. IDA countries commonly have high incidences of extreme poverty and considerable long-standing development challenges, although there are also important differences among low-income countries, countries facing fragile and conflict-affected situations (FCS), and small states. Common characteristics in IDA countries include weak institutions, limited fiscal space (with modest revenue capacity and high levels of debt vulnerability), persistent current account deficits, heavy reliance on external financial flows, exports concentrated in a handful of products, shallow financial markets, and sizable human capital and infrastructure needs.

Evolution of activity and inflation. Growth slowed across IDA countries in 2020 to 0.3 percent, the lowest annual rate recorded since the early 1980s. Within this average, output contracted in IDA FCS and (at a double-digit average rates) in IDA small states. Per capita income growth has also rebounded much more weakly in IDA countries since 2021 than in other emerging market and developing economies (EMDEs). Average headline inflation rose further in IDA countries in 2020-22 than in other EMDEs, peaking in mid-2022, with rising food prices contributing to increased hunger.

Impact of crises on IDA countries. The crises in 2020-23 took a massive toll on IDA countries. Output fell 4 percent below prepandemic trends in 2020, and output losses are projected to reach 5.7 percent in 2024. By the end of 2024, IDA countries are expected to have experienced their weakest half decade of growth since the early 1990s. The rate of per capita income growth over 2020-24 is expected to be almost identical to that of advanced economies, and half of IDA countries—the largest share since the start of this century—will have been growing more slowly in per capita terms, on average, than wealthy economies over that period. This will widen the income gap between these countries and advanced economies.

Moreover, progress on poverty reduction has stalled in IDA countries: the pandemic alone erased three years of progress in reducing the rate of extreme poverty. Poverty is expected to fall only very gradually in these countries through 2030. It is estimated that 26.5 percent of the population in IDA countries was living in extreme poverty in 2023, more than eight times the proportion in the rest of the world. About 651 million people in IDA countries faced food insecurity in 2023, nearly double the 2019 number and 92 percent of the global total.

Near-term prospects. Growth is expected to increase modestly in IDA countries during 2024-25, but overall, activity is projected to remain subdued relative to their 2010-19 average growth rate. Inflation is forecast to moderate further but to remain higher than in other EMDEs and above IDA countries' prepandemic average. Although there are signs of a tentative recovery in trade and investment growth, they are expected to remain muted relative to development needs. In sum, growth in the next few years is expected to be insufficient to significantly improve the development trajectory of IDA countries.

Risks. The key risk to the outlook for IDA countries is that the current stagnation becomes more protracted. Persistent weak income growth could deepen reversals in progress. IDA countries are especially susceptible to the increased numbers and severity of natural disasters associated with climate change. IDA FCS are particularly vulnerable to new shocks given their weak fundamentals. The highly challenging external environment magnifies the risks: weaker-than-expected global growth, an escalation in geopolitical tensions, fragmentation of trade and investment networks, or an extended period of tighter global financial conditions could further darken prospects for IDA countries.

Reasons for optimism. While IDA countries face a wide range of challenges, there are also factors in their favor. First, progress is possible. Since 2000, a dozen countries have successfully graduated from the IDA (that is, they once were eligible for IDA resources, but their economies have grown sufficiently that they no longer meet the eligibility criteria). Large economies such as China, India, and the Republic of Korea were once IDA countries. Second, many IDA countries have rich stores of natural resources and favorable demographic profiles, although they need to manage both of these advantages effectively to realize their potential. IDA countries possess abundant supplies of various commodities, with many having substantial reserves of minerals critical to the global energy transition. Working-age populations in IDA countries are expected to expand over the next half century, unlike those in the rest of the world. If these advantages can be harnessed, they should significantly benefit economic growth and development. Third, experience shows that it is possible to accelerate investment growth and deliver transformative structural change by undertaking comprehensive policy reforms.

National policy priorities. To confront these challenges and risks effectively, IDA countries need to implement well-designed and ambitious policies, focused particularly on boosting investment growth. These should include policies to durably improve fiscal and external imbalances, secure macroeconomic stability, and advance an array of structural reforms—to strengthen institutions, better manage natural resources, boost human capital, enhance gender equality and youth inclusion, and combat climate change, among other things. Implementation of such policies has the potential to spark an extended period of strong investment growth, which is necessary to meet substantial investment needs, promote income growth, accelerate poverty reduction, and address infrastructure gaps (including those related to climate change and digital transformation) in these countries.

Global support. Strong and sustained financial support from the international community is vital to help contain the risks IDA countries face, address crises that occur should these risks materialize, and unlock opportunities. It is also critical that the global community redouble international cooperation efforts, particularly those in support of IDA countries, on several fronts: to counter the impacts of climate change, via coordinated mitigation and adaptation efforts; to combat fragmentation and support international trade and investment, as a significant growth engine for many IDA countries; to ensure more timely and effective debt restructurings for developing countries that need them; and to buttress IDA countries' domestic development efforts, with a view to building shared and sustainable prosperity. Effective global support and cooperation are essential for IDA countries—and progress in IDA countries is critical for long-term global peace and prosperity.

CHAPTER 2
Characteristics of IDA Countries

The 75 economies eligible for grants and low-interest loans from the IDA represent nearly one-fourth of the global population, yet they account for more than 70 percent of the world's extreme poor. These countries face significant development challenges, particularly in respect to health, education, and infrastructure, and they are especially vulnerable as a result of violent conflict-affected situations and exposure to natural disasters. Limited fiscal space, weak institutional capacity, and underdeveloped financial sectors further complicate efforts to overcome these challenges.

Commonalities

Each IDA country is unique, yet many share common characteristics that tend to hinder their development efforts and increase their vulnerability to shocks.

Low per capita income. Most IDA countries have notably low income levels. A primary criterion for eligibility for IDA assistance is relative poverty. Thirty-one of the 75 IDA countries have annual per capita gross national incomes below $1,315.[1] Other IDA countries surpass this income threshold but lack the creditworthiness to borrow from the International Bank for Reconstruction and Development (IBRD).[2] One-third of IDA countries are classified as low-income countries (LICs).[3] The remaining two-thirds predominantly comprise lower-middle-income countries. A few IDA-eligible small states have higher income levels (figure 2.1.A).

Large population, small share of global output. With an aggregate 1.9 billion inhabitants, IDA countries are home to almost one-quarter of the global population—a share that is growing. Geographically, more than half of IDA countries are in Sub-Saharan Africa, and nearly 20 percent are in East Asia and

---

[1] The IDA used this threshold of $1,315 for the fiscal year that ended June 30, 2024. Some IDA-eligible countries, such as Nigeria and Pakistan, are also considered creditworthy for some borrowing from the International Bank for Reconstruction and Development (IBRD); these are referred to as "blend" countries, and they are also among the 75 countries currently eligible for IDA resources and considered in this study. Table A.1 provides a list of classifications of IDA countries.

[2] In 2023, annual per capita income in IDA countries ranged from $222 in Burundi to $30,899 in Guyana. Annual per capita income in Guyana has surged in recent years, from $6,309 in 2019, owing to the extraction of recently discovered oil. Across emerging market and developing economy regions, Sub-Saharan Africa has the lowest annual per capita income, averaging $1,352, and Europe and Central Asia has the highest, at $2,273.

[3] All LICs, with the exception of the Democratic People's Republic of Korea, are eligible for IDA resources.

FIGURE 2.1 **Characteristics of IDA countries**

IDA countries have low per capita incomes and high rates of extreme poverty. They account for almost a quarter of the global population but contribute only a small fraction to global output. Many IDA countries are in Sub-Saharan Africa, where most of the world's poor reside.

A. Classifications

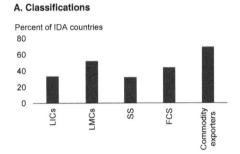

B. Regional distribution

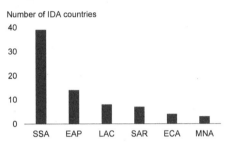

C. Share of global output, 2015-23

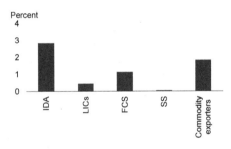

D. Extreme poverty across groups of IDA countries, 2023

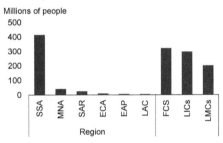

Sources: Mahler and Lakner (2022); World Bank, Poverty and Inequality Platform; World Bank.
Note: EAP = IDA countries in East Asia and Pacific; ECA = IDA countries in Europe and Central Asia; FCS = IDA countries classified as fragile and conflict-affected situations; IDA = IDA countries; LAC = IDA countries in Latin America and the Caribbean; LICs = IDA countries classified as low-income countries; LMCs = IDA countries classified as low- and middle-income countries; MNA = IDA countries in the Middle East and North Africa; SAR = IDA countries in South Asia; SS = IDA countries classified as small states; SSA = IDA countries in Sub-Saharan Africa.
A. Classification is for the 2023-24 fiscal year.
D. Bars show the number of people living below the definition of extreme poverty of $2.15 a day. Data from Mahler and Lakner (2022) and the World Bank's Poverty and Inequality Platform.

the Pacific, where many are small states (figure 2.1.B). In South Asia, all countries except India are IDA countries. Despite their significant combined population, IDA countries collectively account for just 3 percent of global output (figure 2.1.C).[4]

Widespread extreme poverty, heightened fragility. More than 70 percent of the world's extreme poor reside in IDA countries, with nearly 500 million people living below the extreme poverty line of $2.15 per person per day in 2023. This level of poverty affected, on average, 26.5 percent of the population

---

[4] LICs and countries facing fragile and conflict-affected situations contribute a mere 0.5 percent and 1.1 percent to global GDP, respectively. IDA's small states have a marginal share of global output, and IDA's commodity exporters collectively account for 1.9 percent of global GDP.

FIGURE 2.2 IDA countries: Outward orientation and vulnerability to natural disasters

IDA countries exhibit relatively low levels of trade openness coupled with significant concentrations in goods exports. The number of people affected and the substantial damage these disasters cause underscore IDA countries' vulnerability to climate change.

A. Average trade openness and goods exports concentration, 2021-22

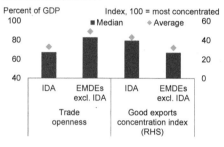

B. Average vulnerability to climate-change-related risk by region, 2017-21 average

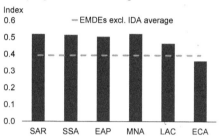

C. Average number of people affected by natural disasters by region, 2013-22

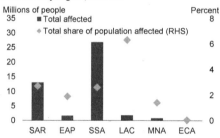

D. Annual average costs of natural disasters

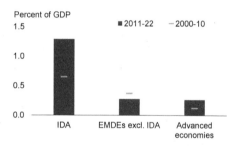

Sources: EM-DAT (database); GRD—Government Revenue Dataset; Notre Dame Global Adaptation Initiative; United Nations Conference on Trade and Development; WDI database; World Bank.

Note: EAP = IDA countries in East Asia and Pacific; ECA = IDA countries in Europe and Central Asia; IDA = IDA countries; LAC = IDA countries in Latin America and the Caribbean; MNA = IDA countries in the Middle East and North Africa; RHS = right-hand scale; SAR = IDA countries in South Asia; SSA = IDA countries in Sub-Saharan Africa.

A. "Trade openness" shows the sum of exports and imports. Sample includes 49 IDA countries and 63 EMDEs excluding IDA countries. The goods exports concentration index measures the degree to which a country's exports are composed of a small number of commodities. Sample includes 74 IDA countries and 78 EMDEs excluding IDA countries.

B. Aggregates are computed using 2015 GDPs as weights.

B.C. Regional aggregates include only IDA countries.

in IDA countries in 2023, a rate more than eight times higher than the average of 3.1 percent observed in the rest of the world. Most of those living in extreme poverty are in Sub-Saharan Africa (figure 2.1.D).

Moreover, heightened vulnerabilities attributable to institutional fragility, social unrest, and conflict characterize many IDA countries. Thirty-three IDA countries are classified as fragile and conflict-affected situations (FCS), with 324 million individuals living in extreme poverty within this group. In total, an estimated 35 percent or more of the population in IDA FCS endured extreme poverty in 2023, and 43 percent of people in IDA LICs live in extreme poverty. A significant number of IDA countries are categorized as LICs, FCS, or both.

Less open to trade. IDA countries engage in less international trade, relative to their gross domestic products (GDPs), than other emerging market and developing economies (EMDEs) (figure 2.2.A). Specifically, trade-to-GDP ratios averaged about 66 percent over 2021-22 in IDA countries, less than the 82 percent of GDP in other EMDEs. This gap is even more pronounced in IDA LICs, where trade openness averages only 57 percent of GDP. Conversely, IDA small states demonstrate significantly higher levels of trade openness, exceeding 93 percent of GDP on average.

Undiversified production and exports. IDA countries tend to have output and exports concentrated in a narrow range of products. On average, about 40 percent of goods exports from IDA countries are from a single sector, well above the 27 percent average in other EMDEs. As chapter 7 documents, most IDA countries have significant stores of natural resources and rely heavily on income from commodities, with 52 IDA countries classified as commodity exporters.[5] However, IDA's commodity importers and exporters alike rely heavily on food and fuel imports, highlighting the vulnerabilities and challenges they face from the volatility of commodity prices. Many IDA countries, particularly those that are small states, attract substantial tourist flows, with more than half of IDA small states classified as tourism reliant.[6]

Exposure to climate-change-related and other natural disasters. Vulnerability to natural disasters, those related to climate change as well as other types, is a pressing concern for IDA countries. Climate change in particular poses growing threats to lives, livelihoods, and economic stability in these countries (figure 2.2.B; Casey, Fried, and Goode 2023). Because of climate change, natural disasters are increasing in frequency and severity worldwide, with people in IDA countries bearing the brunt of extreme weather events (figure 2.2.C).

These countries sustain substantial economic losses from natural disasters that have risen significantly over time, averaging 1.3 percent of GDP over 2011-22—considerably higher than in other EMDEs (figure 2.2.D). LICs and small states, often with limited resources, are particularly vulnerable to the effects of climate change, including droughts, floods, and rising sea levels (Jafino et al. 2020; World Bank 2023). Climate change also disproportionately affects the agricultural sector, which is crucial for many IDA countries. Beyond economic losses, extreme weather events can significantly affect food security and livelihoods, especially in FCS (FAO et al. 2023).

---

[5] Among IDA countries, 11 are energy exporters, with 10 primarily exporters of oil; 17 are metal exporters; and 28 are categorized as commodity exporters because of sizable shares of agricultural exports.

[6] A country is classified as tourism reliant if its inbound tourism expenditure as a share of GDP during 2015-19 ranked above the third quartile of shares in all EMDEs, based on United Nations World Tourism Organization data.

FIGURE 2.3 **IDA countries: Human development indicators and infrastructure**

Despite progress across various human development indicators in recent decades, IDA countries continue to trail other economies, particularly in regard to maternal and early childhood mortality

A. Life expectancy and maternal mortality

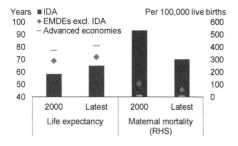

B. Early childhood stunting and mortality rate

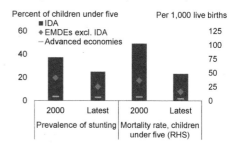

C. Access to infrastructure

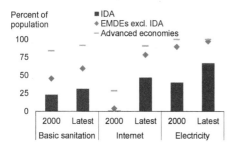

D. Institutional quality

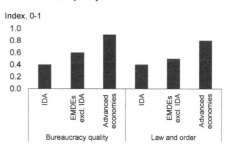

E. Informal output, 2010-20

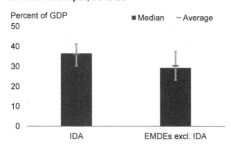

F. Government revenues and expenditures, 2023

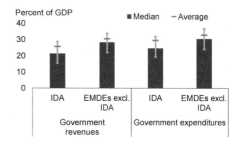

Sources: Elgin et al. (2021); ICRG database; WDI database; WEO database; WHO database; World Bank.
Note: EMDEs = emerging market and developing economies; IDA = IDA countries.
A. Data show simple averages for an unbalanced sample of 74 IDA countries, 79 EMDEs excluding IDA countries, and 38 advanced economies. "Latest" refers to 2021 for life expectancy and to 2020 for maternal mortality.
B. Data for mortality rate show simple averages for 75 IDA countries, 79 EMDEs excluding IDA countries, and 36 advanced economies, and those for stunting show simple averages for 70 IDA countries, 72 EMDEs excluding IDA countries, and 14 advanced economies. "Latest" refers to 2021 for mortality rate and to 2022 for stunting.
C. Average percentage of population, based on World Development Indicators data. "Latest" refers to 2021 for electricity and internet, and 2022 for basic sanitation. Data for electricity show simple averages for an unbalanced sample of 74 IDA countries, 79 EMDEs excluding IDA countries, and 37 advanced economies. Those for internet show simple averages for an unbalanced sample of 64 IDA countries, 75 EMDEs excluding IDA countries, and 37 advanced economies. Those for basic sanitation show simple averages of an unbalanced sample of 42 IDA countries, 47 EMDEs excluding IDA countries, and 34 advanced economies.
D. Panel shows *International Country Risk Guide* scores. Indexes are normalized to unity. Sample includes 38 IDA countries, 62 EMDEs excluding IDA countries, and 36 advanced economies.
E. Estimates of informal output based on calculations from a dynamic general equilibrium model. Bars show the results for 53 IDA countries and 68 other EMDEs excluding IDA countries. Panel shows 2010-20 average. Whiskers show interquartile range.
F. Data on general government total revenues and expenditures are shown for 2023. Whiskers show interquartile range. Sample includes 71 IDA countries and 77 EMDEs excluding IDA countries.

Pervasive development gaps despite progress. IDA countries have shown significant progress on human development indicators in recent decades. Life expectancy, for example, rose from 58 to 65 years in IDA countries between 2000 and 2021. Maternal mortality rates decreased by about half, from one in every 188 live births in 2000 to one in 332 in the latest data (2020). Nevertheless, key indicators also reveal persistent gaps with other EMDEs (figures 2.3.A and 2.3.B). In IDA countries, life expectancy is approximately seven years lower than in other EMDEs, maternal mortality rates are five times higher, and malnutrition and child mortality rates remain high. IDA countries also lag in access to physical and digital infrastructure: although access to basic sanitation, electricity, and the internet has improved substantially in IDA countries since 2000, it is still much lower than that in other EMDEs (figure 2.3.C).

Weak institutions. IDA countries generally have weaker institutions than other EMDEs (figure 2.3.D). This institutional weakness is broad in scope, including tenuous legal capacity for protecting property rights, the persistence of political violence, state and market failures, weak governance, and corruption. Moreover, the presence of important natural resource endowments in many IDA countries—a potential boon—can impede economic diversification while breeding corruption and conflict (Gill et al. 2014; World Bank 2017). These issues heighten country risk profiles, hindering capital inflows. Limited institutional capacity also affects data availability and quality, complicating policy design and implementation.

High levels of informality, limited fiscal space. In the typical IDA country, the informal economy accounts for a sizable share of GDP: 36 percent over 2010-20, compared with 29 percent in other EMDEs (figure 2.3.E). This widespread informality constrains efforts to mobilize government revenue, which in turn hampers governments' capacity to deliver key public services (figure 2.3.F; Gaspar, Jaramillo, and Wingender 2016). In 2021, tax revenue in IDA countries averaged only 11.9 percent of GDP (much lower than the 17.1 percent in other EMDEs), significantly limiting the resources available for public investment and social programs. Consequently, spending on critical sectors like health and education remains notably lower than that in other EMDEs, averaging 1.6 and 3.6 percent of GDP, respectively, over 2000-20 across IDA countries—significantly below the 2.9 and 4.1 percent averages in other EMDEs.

Persistent twin deficits, underdeveloped financial sectors. In many IDA countries, sizable and persistent twin (fiscal and current account) deficits prevail. Elevated levels of debt often accompany these deficits. IDA countries rely heavily on external sources—including remittances—to meet their financing needs. Moreover, they tend to have underdeveloped domestic financial sectors, with limited capacity for conducting basic intermediation transactions linking savers and borrowers. Shallow and illiquid financial systems, lacking diverse instruments, leave IDA countries ill equipped to absorb and mitigate the impact of adverse shocks (Sahay et al. 2015).

References

Casey, G., S. Fried, and E. Goode. 2023. "Projecting the Impact of Rising Temperatures: The Role of Macroeconomic Dynamics." CESifo Working Paper 10375, Center for Economic Studies, ifo Institute, Munich.

Elgin, C., M. A. Kose, F. Ohnsorge, and S. Yu. 2021. "Growing Apart or Moving Together? Synchronization of Informal and Formal Economy Business Cycles." In *The Long Shadow of Informality: Challenges and Policies*, edited by F. Ohnsorge and S. Yu, 93-119. Washington, DC: World Bank.

EM-DAT: The International Disaster Database (accessed February 4, 2024). https://www.emdat.be/.

FAO (Food and Agriculture Organization of the United Nations), IFAD (International Fund for Agricultural Development), UNICEF (United Nations Children's Fund), WFP (World Food Programme), and WHO (World Health Organization). 2023. "The State of Food Security and Nutrition in the World 2023. Urbanization, Agrifood Systems Transformation and Healthy Diets across the Rural—Urban Continuum." FAO, Rome.

Gaspar, V., L. Jaramillo, and P. Wingender. 2016. "Tax Capacity and Growth: Is There a Tipping Point?" IMF Working Paper 16/243, International Monetary Fund, Washington, DC.

Gill, I. S., I. Izvorski, W. van Eeghen, and D. De Rosa. 2014. *Diversified Development: Making the Most of Natural Resources in Eurasia.* Washington, DC: World Bank.

GRD—Government Revenue Dataset (accessed February 17, 2024). https://www.wider.unu.edu/project/grd-government-revenue-dataset.

ICRG (International Country Risk Guide) database (accessed February 17, 2024). https://www.prsgroup.com/explore-our-products/icrg/.

Jafino, B. A., B. Walsh, J. Rozenberg, and S. Hallegatte. 2020. "Revised Estimates of the Impact of Climate Change on Extreme Poverty by 2030." Policy Research Working Paper 9417, World Bank, Washington, DC.

Mahler, D. G., and C. Lakner. 2022. "The Impact of COVID-19 on Global Inequality and Poverty." Policy Research Working Paper 10198, World Bank, Washington, DC.

Sahay, R., M. Čihak, P. N'Diaye, A. Barajas, R. Bi, D. Ayala, Y. Gao, et al. 2015. "Rethinking Financial Deepening: Stability and Growth in Emerging Markets." IMF Staff Discussion Note 15/08, International Monetary Fund, Washington, DC.

WDI (World Development Indicators) database (accessed March 29, 2024). https://datatopics.worldbank.org/world-development-indicators/.

WHO (World Health Organization) database (["Maternal Mortality Ratio"]; accessed February 5, 2024). https://www.who.int/data/gho/indicator-metadata-registry/imrdetails/26.

World Bank. 2017. *World Development Report: Governance and the Law.* Washington, DC: World Bank.

World Bank. 2023. "Small States: Overlapping Crises, Multiple Challenges." In *Global Economic Prospects*, January. Washington, DC: World Bank.

In 2020, during the global recession triggered by the COVID-19 pandemic, gross domestic product (GDP) growth in IDA countries fell to its slowest pace since the early 1980s. Further crises associated with the Russian Federation's invasion of Ukraine, a sharp increase in global inflation, the associated tightening of monetary policy, and constrained financing options have further impeded the subsequent recovery.

Output growth

Growth in IDA countries fell to 0.3 percent in 2020—the slowest pace recorded since the early 1980s—as sharply lower external demand, a collapse in tourism activity, and weaker capital flows worsened disruptions to domestic activity associated with the COVID-19 pandemic (table 3.1; figures 3.1.A and 3.1.B). Falling prices of industrial commodities—particularly oil—also hampered activity in some IDA commodity exporters. The initial impact of the pandemic varied considerably among groups of IDA countries: in IDA low-income countries (LICs), growth slowed to 1.5 percent in 2020—about one-third its 2010-19 average pace; in IDA countries facing fragile and conflict-affected situations (FCS), output contracted by 1.5 percent, reflecting these countries' weak state capacity and limited fiscal space. Hardest hit were IDA small states, with output shrinking by 12.4 percent in 2020 as international travel and tourism collapsed.[1]

In 2021, IDA countries recorded rebounded much more weakly from the pandemic than other emerging market and developing economies (EMDEs). Growth in IDA countries strengthened from 0.3 percent in 2020 to 4.7 percent in 2021, supported by improvements in global trade and commodity prices. In other EMDEs, by contrast, growth rose to 7.3 percent in 2021, after a 1.5 percent contraction in 2020, as economic reopening and vaccine deployment in some larger economies supported a recovery in consumer and business

---

[1] The initial impact of the pandemic also varied considerably among IDA countries. Output fell by nearly one-third in Maldives, one-quarter in St. Lucia, and one-fifth in Cabo Verde in 2020, as tourism plummeted. But more diversified economies, such as Bangladesh and Ethiopia, experienced relatively resilient growth in 2020. In Guyana, idiosyncratic factors, such as the discovery of crude oil, resulted in a pronounced pickup in growth in 2020.

[2] In some IDA countries, such as Honduras, the rebound in growth in 2021 also reflected recoveries from the previous year's hurricanes.

TABLE 3.1 GDP growth

	2010-19 average	2020	2021	2022	2023e	2024f	2025f
IDA	4.8	0.3	4.7	4.2	3.7	4.3	4.5
IDA only	5.6	0.9	4.6	4.8	4.3	5.1	5.3
IDA blend	4.0	-0.3	4.8	3.5	2.8	3.3	3.5
IDA low-income countries	4.7	1.5	4.1	5.0	3.8	4.9	5.3
IDA middle-income countries	4.9	0.0	4.8	3.8	3.4	3.9	4.3
IDA FCS	4.2	-1.5	2.4	3.9	2.9	3.6	3.8
IDA small states	3.7	-12.4	6.2	8.1	4.5	4.1	4.2
Other aggregates							
Advanced economies[a]		2.0	-4.0	5.5	2.6	1.5	1.4	1.6
EMDEs[a]		5.1	-1.5	7.1	3.7	4.2	3.9	4.1
EMDEs excl. IDA countries		5.1	-1.6	7.3	3.7	4.2	3.8	4.0

Source: World Bank.

Note: "Middle-income countries" includes both lower-middle-income and upper-middle-income countries. World Bank forecasts are frequently updated based on new information. Consequently, projections presented here may differ from those provided in other World Bank documents, even if basic assessments of countries' prospects do not differ at any given date. Aggregate growth rates are calculated using GDP weights at average 2010-19 prices and market exchange rates. Aggregate growth rates exclude Afghanistan, Lebanon, Somalia, the Syrian Arab Republic, and the Republic of Yemen because of a high degree of uncertainty. Aggregate growth rates for IDA small states exclude Guyana. Sample of IDA countries includes 71 economies. e = estimate; excl. = excluding; f = forecast; EMDEs = emerging market and developing economies; FCS = fragile and conflict-affected situations; GDP = gross domestic product; IDA = International Development Association; IDA only = countries eligible only for IDA resources; IDA blend = countries eligible for both IDA and International Bank for Reconstruction and Development resources.
[a] The data presented for advanced economies and EMDEs reflect preliminary working assumptions and are subject to change. The World Bank Group publishes official forecasts for advanced economies and EMDEs only in January and June.

confidence, lifted services activity, and buttressed financial market sentiment.[2] Although growth in IDA's small states rebounded to 6.2 percent in 2021, this was still weaker than the recovery in other EMDEs, as services trade remained depressed by continuing travel restrictions.[3] IDA LICs and FCS experienced weaker recovery than the IDA average, with growth reaching only 4.1 percent in LICs and 2.4 percent in FCS. These weaker recoveries reflected very low vaccination rates, limited policy support for demand and activity, and a deterioration in security in many countries (World Bank 2022a).[4]

IDA countries' growth disappointed further in subsequent years, slowing to 4.2 percent in 2022 and an estimated 3.7 percent in 2023. This performance was similar to that of other EMDEs, but well below IDA countries' average growth of 4.8 percent over 2010-19. Weakening domestic demand growth amid sharp rises in the cost of living; tight financial conditions; and worsening conflict, violence, and instability in some cases largely drove the 2023 slowdown. Net

---

[3] Growth in 2021 rebounded more strongly in some tourism-dependent IDA countries, such as Maldives, as a result of earlier economic reopening.

[4] A marked deterioration in security, political stability, or both triggered double-digit contractions in output in 2021 in some IDA countries, including Afghanistan and Myanmar.

FIGURE 3.1 **Macroeconomic developments in IDA countries: Activity**

GDP growth in IDA countries fell to 0.3 percent in 2020: the slowest rate of growth recorded since the early 1980s. Though many IDA countries initially took a smaller hit than other EMDEs, some IDA country groups suffered more. Activity in IDA LICs and FCS disappointed last year, with substantial downgrades to growth estimates in both groups. The recovery in trade growth since 2021 has been muted, though it is forecast to pick up somewhat in the coming years.

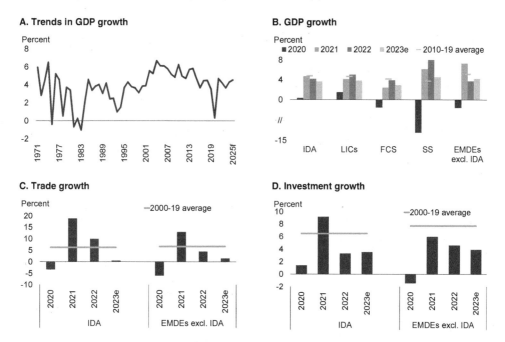

Sources: Haver Analytics; Macro Poverty Outlook database; World Bank.
Note: e = estimate; f = forecast. EMDEs = emerging market and developing economies; FCS = IDA countries classified as fragile and conflict-affected situations; GDP = gross domestic product; IDA = IDA countries; LICs = IDA countries classified as low-income countries; SS = IDA countries classified as small states excluding Guyana.
A. Aggregate calculated using real U.S. dollar GDP weights at average 2010-19 prices and market exchange rates.
C. "Trade" refers to trade in goods and services, which is measured as the average of export and import volumes.
D. "Investment growth" refers to gross fixed capital formation. Investment growth data are from the January 2024 edition of the *Global Economic Prospects* report.

exports contributed positively to growth in 2023, but owing to import compression, reflecting weak domestic demand, rather than to burgeoning exports.

Although the April 2024 estimate for growth in IDA countries in 2023 is above the January 2024 estimate, for almost half of IDA LICs and FCS, growth estimates have been revised down. Pervasive violence and political instability exacerbated the challenging economic and humanitarian situations in many of these countries in 2023, weighing on growth.[5] Additionally, extreme weather

---

[5] For instance, Sudan faced significant deterioration, with a resumption of conflict damaging the country's industrial base, and Niger suffered a pronounced decline, mostly due to a July coup and the subsequent international sanctions.

events have had catastrophic consequences in several IDA countries, especially in LICs in the Sahel region, which is warming faster than the global average and is also particularly susceptible to desertification (World Bank 2022b).

Trade and investment growth

Trade and investment growth were both volatile over 2020-23 in IDA countries. After trade in IDA countries contracted 3.3 percent in 2020—the steepest fall since 1981—it rebounded robustly over 2021-22 (figure 3.1.C). However, this rebound was short-lived, with trade growth slowing to only 0.5 percent in 2023, well below the 6.3 percent average over 2000-19, owing to a weak external environment. Investment growth in IDA countries followed a similar pattern: it slumped to 1.4 percent in 2020, the lowest in more than a decade (figure 3.1.D). There was a strong cyclical rebound in 2021, but investment growth was subdued in 2022 and 2023, at about 3 percentage points below the 2000-19 average in each year, reflecting the multiple crises of 2020-23 (World Bank 2024).

Inflation and food insecurity

Surging inflation impeded the recovery from the pandemic. Headline inflation in IDA countries increased significantly from a higher base than in other EMDEs, reaching its highest annual rate since 2008 in 2022 (figure 3.2.A). Russia's invasion of Ukraine in February 2022 precipitated a significant upswing in energy prices and pushed global food prices to all-time highs. This inflationary spike eroded food affordability in many IDA countries (figure 3.2.B). Currency depreciations in a number of countries added to inflationary pressures.

The effects of inflation are not felt equally, including within IDA countries. Inflation tends to increase poverty and inequality (Gill and Nagle 2022). Low- and middle-income households are generally more vulnerable to high inflation than wealthier households, as a result of differences in their assets, incomes, and consumption baskets. The very poorest, who often have limited wage income and assets and rely, for example, on subsistence farming, will nevertheless still be affected by inflation.

Russia's invasion of Ukraine had pronounced impacts on IDA countries, not only through higher commodity prices, but also because of their dependence on energy and food imports from the two countries. Although elevated global commodity prices benefited some exporters of energy and metals, increases in energy and fertilizer costs largely offset the benefits of higher prices for agricultural exporters (figure 3.2.C). Moreover, the surge in commodity prices weighed on private consumption in IDA countries as a result of high food and

FIGURE 3.2 Inflation, commodity prices, and food insecurity in IDA countries

Inflation has slowed in IDA countries but still remains elevated, while food insecurity has surged alongside higher food prices and increased conflict and violence.

A. Annual consumer price inflation

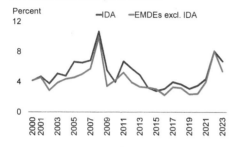

B. Food price inflation

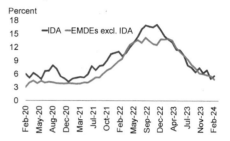

C. Commodity prices

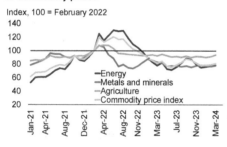

D. Food insecurity

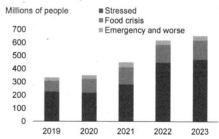

Sources: GRFC (database); Haver Analytics; Macro Poverty Outlook database.

Note: EMDEs = emerging market and developing economies; excl. = excluding; IDA = IDA countries.

A. Panel shows median year-over-year headline inflation. Unbalanced sample of up to 70 IDA countries and 70 EMDEs excluding IDA countries.

B. Panel shows year-over-year group median inflation for the food component of the consumer price index for up to 31 IDA countries and 63 EMDEs excluding IDA countries. Last observation is February 2024.

C. Data are measured in U.S. dollars. Last observation is March 2024.

D. "Stressed" households cannot cover some essential nonfood costs without resorting to stress-coping strategies. "Food crisis" households either experience food shortages with high acute malnutrition or meet minimal food needs through significant asset depletion or crisis-coping actions. "Emergency" households face severe food shortages, resulting in very high acute malnutrition and increased mortality, or bridge major food gaps solely through emergency livelihood strategies and asset liquidation. "Worse" households suffer from an extreme shortage of food and coping mechanisms, leading to starvation, death, destitution, and critically high acute malnutrition. Sample includes data for up to 50 IDA countries.

fuel shares in their consumption baskets. As a result, the recovery stemming from a gradual waning of the pandemic and increased export earnings was muted in IDA countries, as rapidly climbing costs of living dampened domestic demand. These developments led to increased hunger: 651 million people in IDA countries faced food insecurity in 2023, almost double the number in 2019 (figure 3.2.D).

Fiscal balances and public debt

Public debt had already built up significantly in IDA countries prior to the pandemic, and increased budget deficits since 2020 have exacerbated debt

FIGURE 3.3 **Fiscal accounts in IDA countries**

Budget deficits grew less in IDA countries than in other EMDEs in 2020 but have remained elevated since then. By 2023, government-debt-to-GDP ratios in IDA countries had surged by 6.7 percentage points compared with those in 2019: about three times the increase in other EMDEs. Sovereign spreads have widened significantly for IDA countries since 2022, and bond issuances have dipped. Net interest payments as a share of revenues have increased in IDA countries more rapidly than in other EMDEs; about half of IDA countries are in or at high risk of debt distress.

A. Government budget deficits

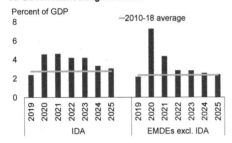

B. Government debt

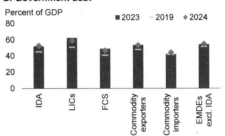

C. Sovereign bond spreads

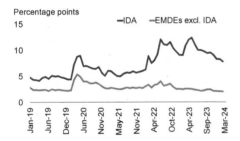

D. Government bond issuance by non-investment-grade countries

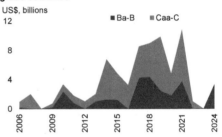

E. Net interest payments

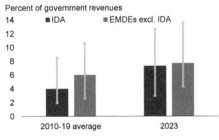

F. Risk of external debt distress

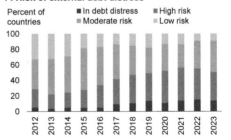

Sources: Dealogic; J.P. Morgan; Moody's Analytics; WEO database; World Bank.

Note: EMDEs = emerging market and developing economies; FCS = IDA countries classified as fragile and conflict-affected situations; GDP = gross domestic product; IDA = IDA countries; IMF = International Monetary Fund; LICs = IDA countries classified as low-income countries.

A. Panel shows median general government net lending and borrowing for unbalanced sample of up to 74 IDA countries and 79 EMDEs excluding IDA countries.

B. Panel shows median general government gross debt for a sample of 67 IDA countries, 20 IDA low-income countries, 27 IDA countries facing fragile and conflict-affected situations, 48 IDA commodity exporters, and 76 EMDEs excluding IDA countries.

C. Panel shows median of J.P. Morgan's Emerging Market Bond Index spreads for an unbalanced panel of up to 13 IDA countries and 48 EMDEs excluding IDA countries. Last observation is March 31, 2024.

D. Panel shows rolling 12-month totals for bond issuance by IDA countries, categorized by Moody's ratings for long-term foreign currency sovereign credit. Last observation is February 2024.

E. "Net interest payments" are the difference between primary balances and overall fiscal balances. Aggregates are computed with government revenues in U.S. dollars as weights. Bars show simple average for up to 69 IDA countries and 71 EMDEs excluding IDA countries. Whiskers indicate interquartile range.

F. Panel shows share of IDA countries eligible to access the IMF's concessional lending facilities by level of external debt distress, based on IMF-World Bank debt sustainability analysis list as of November 2023. Unbalanced panel of up to 67 IDA countries. Eritrea is excluded owing to the unavailability of the latest debt sustainability analysis. St. Lucia is excluded since it currently uses the IMF's Sovereign Risk and Debt Sustainability Framework for Market Access Countries.

burdens (figure 3.3.A; Kose, Ohnsorge, and Sugawara 2023). A sizable share of the government debt that IDA countries accumulated over 2010-23 was accrued before the pandemic, with persistent budget deficits fueling the accrual. Fiscal support packages implemented during the pandemic, though smaller than in other EMDEs owing to IDA countries' preexisting fiscal constraints, nevertheless sharply increased deficits, to 4.5 percent of GDP on average in 2020 (a rise of about 2 percentage points from 2019) and persisting at 4.2 percent of GDP as of 2023. IDA countries have undertaken much less fiscal adjustment since 2020 than other EMDEs, in which fiscal balances edged closer to prepandemic averages in 2022-23.

Widening fiscal deficits have led to a sharp increase in public debt, relative to GDP, in IDA countries. By 2023, the median government-debt-to-GDP ratio in IDA countries had risen by 6.7 percentage points since 2019—about three times the increase in other EMDEs—to more than 50 percent of GDP (figure 3.3.B). Particularly striking is the escalation of public debt in LICs, where it went up by about 12 percentage points of GDP between 2019 and 2023. The recent rise in debt-to-GDP ratios has been widespread across IDA countries, occurring in nearly 70 percent of them between 2019 and 2023. The rise in government budget deficits in response to the pandemic reversed fiscal consolidation plans across IDA countries: initial forecasts back in 2018 had in fact projected a decrease in government debt, from 50 percent of GDP to 42.3 percent in 2023, in the median IDA country.

Elevated costs of borrowing have magnified debt challenges. Synchronized increases of policy interest rates in many advanced economies in response to high inflation led to much tighter global financing conditions, with significant increases in borrowing costs for IDA countries. The median sovereign bond spread (the difference between the yield on U.S. Treasury securities and what a country pays on an equivalent issuance) for IDA countries rose from 4.7 percentage points in 2019 to a peak of 12.4 percentage points in May 2023, before falling back to 7.8 percentage points in March 2024. This contrasts with the relative stability of sovereign bond spreads for other EMDEs in this period (figure 3.3.C). IDA countries with weak credit ratings have been particularly marginalized in global capital markets.[6] Prohibitively high financing costs shut many IDA countries out of international capital markets and led to minimal bond issuance between 2022 and early 2024, the longest issuance drought since

---

[6] The sovereign bonds of 15 IDA countries had weak credit ratings as of May 2024: Cameroon, Democratic Republic of Congo, Republic of Congo, Ethiopia, Ghana, Lao People's Democratic Republic, Maldives, Mali, Mozambique, Niger, Nigeria, Pakistan, Solomon Islands, Sri Lanka, and Zambia.

the global recession in 2009 (figure 3.3.D; Kenworthy, Kose, and Perevalov 2024).

The rising proportion of government revenues allocated to interest payments in IDA countries also offers evidence of the fiscal strains they are experiencing. The combination of weak growth, high levels of government debt, and elevated interest rates has led to a sharp increase in net interest payments relative to government revenues in IDA countries, to 7.3 percent in 2023. This represents a surge of 3.3 percentage points from prepandemic averages: a much sharper increase than the 1.7 percentage points observed in other EMDEs (figure 3.3.E). These increased interest payments are diverting crucial resources from essential government outlays on education, health, and infrastructure; IDA countries already lag spending in comparison to other EMDEs in these areas, thus further limiting their long-term growth prospects. In some heavily indebted IDA countries, interest payments now surpass historical average spending on health care, underscoring the severity of these countries' financing problems and their detrimental effects on public services and development initiatives.

The share of IDA countries in, or at risk of, debt distress has increased sharply in recent years. More than half of IDA countries for which the World Bank and International Monetary Fund have conducted debt sustainability analyses—34 out of 67—are either in acute debt distress or at high risk thereof (figure 3.3.F). This share was less than one-quarter in 2013. It rose significantly in the years before the pandemic and in 2021.

External balances

In addition to fiscal pressures, external imbalances present significant challenges for IDA countries. The median IDA country had a current account deficit of 4.8 percent of GDP in 2023, markedly higher than the 1.6 percent of GDP recorded in other EMDEs (figure 3.4.A). IDA LICs have substantial current account deficits, at 6.0 percent of GDP. After widening during 2020-22, primarily owing to soaring import bills driven by higher commodity prices, current account deficits in IDA countries are not expected to narrow significantly over the projected horizon. In fact, in IDA FCS, current account deficits are expected to widen sharply, reaching 4.6 percent of GDP by 2025.

Borrowing conditions in IDA countries have worsened as their financing needs have increased, to the detriment of their fiscal positions. Median gross public financing needs, calculated as the sum of fiscal deficits and short-term government debt stocks, rose by 2.3 percentage points in these countries between 2019 and 2023, to 7.9 percent of GDP (figure 3.4.B). A number of

FIGURE 3.4 **External accounts in IDA countries**

Current account deficits and gross public financing needs have risen since 2020 in IDA countries. The sharp rise in current account deficits partly reflects a surge in fuel and food import bills over the same time period. Financing needs remain elevated alongside tight financing conditions and large fiscal deficits. Foreign capital flows, historically a vital source of financing for IDA countries, fell sharply in 2022. Foreign exchange cover tends to be lower in IDA countries than in other EMDEs.

A. Current account deficits

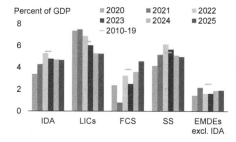

B. Gross public financing needs

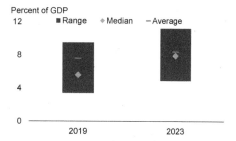

C. Net financial flows

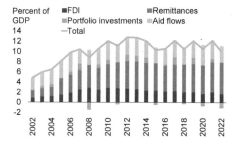

D. Foreign exchange reserves

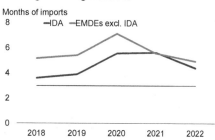

Sources: OECD database; United Nations Conference on Trade and Development; WDI database; WEO database; World Trade Organization; World Bank, KNOMAD (Global Knowledge Partnership on Migration and Development); World Bank.
Note: EMDEs = emerging market and developing economies; excl. = excluding; FCS = IDA countries classified as fragile and conflict-affected situations; FDI = foreign direct investment; GDP = gross domestic product; IDA = IDA countries; LICs = IDA countries classified as low-income countries; SS = IDA countries classified as small states.
A. Sample includes 74 IDA countries, 25 IDA LICs, 32 IDA FCS, 24 IDA SS, and 78 EMDEs excluding IDA countries.
B. Sample includes 31 IDA countries.
C. "Aid flows" refers to total net official development assistance funding.
D. Panel shows median total reserves in months of imports for an unbalanced sample of 55 IDA countries and 49 EMDEs excluding IDA countries. Horizontal line shows three months of imports, often used as a proxy for minimum adequacy of international reserves.

IDA countries—including Burundi, Fiji, The Gambia, Ghana, Kenya, Malawi, Mozambique, Pakistan, Togo, and Zambia—now face financing needs surpassing 10 percent of GDP, underscoring the fiscal pressures these countries face.

Foreign capital inflows have historically played a crucial role in financing in IDA countries, but they dipped in 2022. Net portfolio investment inflows to IDA countries averaged 0.4 percent of GDP between 2019 and 2021, but there was a net outflow of 1.1 percent of GDP in 2022. Foreign direct investment (FDI) flows also declined, from 2.0 percent of GDP in 2019 to 1.7 percent in 2022, continuing a trend in evidence since the 2009 global recession.[7] Excluding remittances, net capital inflows to IDA countries (relative to GDP) have been volatile over the past decade. Although remittances have risen in recent years, other capital flows have been volatile around a gradually declining trend, almost halving from their 2010-13 average. In 2022, total capital flows into IDA countries were the lowest since 2008, no doubt partly owing to the tightening of financial conditions in 2022 (figure 3.4.C). IDA countries also tend to have lower levels of foreign exchange reserves than other EMDEs (figure 3.4.D).

References

Gill, I. S., and P. Nagle. 2022. "Inflation Could Wreak Vengeance on the World's Poor." *Brookings Institution Commentary* (blog), March 18, 2022.

GRFC (Global Report on Food Crises) Database 2016-2024 (accessed February 4, 2024). https://www.fsinplatform.org/our-data.

IMF (International Monetary Fund). 2023. "Geoeconomic Fragmentation and Foreign Direct Investment." In *World Economic Outlook: A Rocky Recovery*, 91-114. Washington, DC: International Monetary Fund. April.

Kenworthy, P., M. A. Kose, and N. Perevalov. 2024. "A Silent Debt Crisis Is Engulfing Developing Economies with Weak Credit Ratings." *World Bank Voices* (blog), February 8, 2024.

Kose, M. A., F. Ohnsorge, and N. Sugawara. 2023. "A Mountain of Debt: Navigating the Legacy of the Pandemic." *Journal of Globalization and Development* 13 (2): 233-68.

Macro Poverty Outlook database (["Poverty Data"]; accessed February 4, 2024). https:// www.worldbank.org/en/publication/macro-poverty-outlook.

OECD (Organisation for Economic Co-operation and Development) database (accessed February 21, 2024). https://www.oecd.org/en/data/indicators/net-oda.html.

Saurav, A., Y. Liu, and A. Sinha. 2020. "Foreign Direct Investment and Employment Outcomes in Developing Countries: A Literature Review of the Effects of FDI on Job Creation and Wages." World Bank, Washington, DC.

---

[7] The decline in FDI is a cause for concern. However, equally troubling is the nature and sectoral distribution of FDI in several IDA countries. In some of these countries, FDI has primarily targeted extractive sectors, resulting in limited backward linkages. This diminishes the direct impact of FDI on job creation and wages, while also constraining its potential spillover effects on domestic enterprises (Saurav, Liu, and Sinha 2020; IMF 2023).

WDI (World Development Indicators) database (accessed March 29, 2024). https://datatopics.worldbank.org/world-development-indicators/.

WEO (World Economic Outlook) database, April 2018 (accessed February 17, 2024). https://www.imf.org/en/Publications/WEO/weo-database/2018/April.

WEO (World Economic Outlook) database, October 2023 (accessed February 27, 2024). https://imf.org/en/Publications/WEO/weo-database/2023/October.

World Bank. 2022a. *Global Economic Prospects.* June. Washington, DC: World Bank.

World Bank. 2022b. *Poverty and Shared Prosperity: Correcting Course.* Washington, DC: World Bank.

World Bank. 2024. *Global Economic Prospects.* January. Washington, DC: World Bank.

CHAPTER 4
Near-Term Growth Prospects: 2024-25

Growth in IDA countries is expected to pick up in 2024-25 as domestic demand recovers, but these countries' recovery is projected to be weak relative to their prepandemic performance.

Output growth

Gross domestic product (GDP) growth in IDA countries is forecast to strengthen in 2024-25 but to remain weaker than its average pace in the decade before the pandemic. Growth is projected to accelerate from an estimated rate of 3.7 percent in 2023 to 4.3 percent in 2024 and 4.5 percent in 2025—outpacing that in other emerging market and developing economies in both years but remaining weaker than the 2010-19 average in IDA countries (figure 4.1.A). This pickup is unlikely to be sufficient to enable IDA countries to make significant progress on poverty reduction.[1]

Domestic and cyclical factors are largely driving the projected pick-up in growth in 2024-25, with demand assumed to strengthen as inflationary pressures recede, interest rates decline, and financial conditions become more accommodative (figure 4.1.B). The contribution from net exports to growth is expected to moderate as a rebound in imports after last year's contraction offsets firming export growth. These forecasts assume that security challenges in several IDA countries moderate, conflicts elsewhere do not escalate, the magnitude of any natural disasters is not unusual, and no new debt crises emerge.

The outlook for growth continues to diverge across IDA countries as of April 2024 (figure 4.1.C). After pronounced weakness in 2023, growth in IDA low-income countries is expected to pick up to an average pace of 5.1 percent a year in 2024-25, 0.5 percentage point lower than January 2024 forecasts. Growth in IDA countries facing fragile and conflict-affected situations (FCS) is also forecast to increase, but only to an average pace of 3.7 percent a year in 2024-25, well

---

[1] Other recent World Bank publications discuss the outlook for Sub-Saharan Africa and South Asia, both regions with large numbers of IDA countries, in detail. They forecast rising GDP growth over the near term but also note that growth rates are expected to remain lower than prepandemic averages, highlighting the weak pass-through from growth to poverty reduction in Africa and modest job creation trends in South Asia (World Bank 2024b, 2024c).

FIGURE 4.1 **Near-term prospects in IDA countries**

Output growth is expected to pick up in IDA countries in 2024-25, driven by strengthening domestic demand. Although inflation is expected to recede in the IDA aggregate over the next two years, it remains elevated in many countries, with inflation reaccelerating in some cases in early 2024.

A. GDP growth

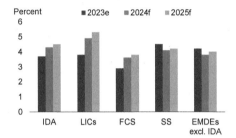

B. Contributions to GDP growth

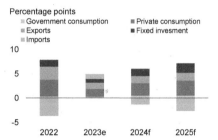

C. Growth across countries, 2024

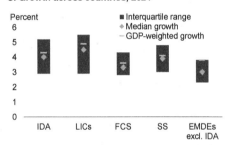

D. Trade growth

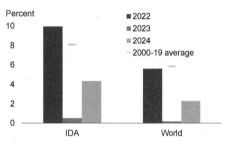

E. 12-month headline consumer price inflation

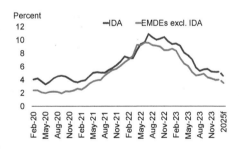

F. Share of countries with increasing monthly inflation

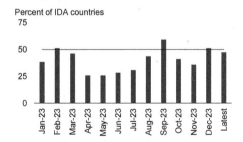

Sources: Haver Analytics; Macro Poverty Outlook database; World Bank.

Note: GDP aggregates are calculated using real U.S. dollar GDP weights at average 2010-19 prices and market exchange rates.
e = estimate; EMDEs = emerging market and developing economies; excl. = excluding; f = forecast; FCS = IDA countries classified as fragile and conflict-affected situations; GDP = gross domestic product; IDA = IDA countries; LICs = IDA countries classified as low-income countries; SS = IDA countries classified as small states excluding Guyana.

B. 37 IDA countries report data on GDP components, which is different from the number of countries reporting data on GDP levels. As such, data for GDP growth derived from components differs from data presented in table A.1.

C. Bars show interquartile range, based on different subgroups of IDA countries.

D. Trade is calculated as an average of exports and imports. World trade projections are based on the January 2024 edition of the *Global Economic Prospects* report. Trade projections for IDA countries are based on current World Bank projections.

E. Panel shows median year-over-year headline inflation. Unbalanced sample of up to 28 IDA countries and 54 EMDEs excluding IDA countries. Dotted line shows forecasts for 2024 and 2025 from World Bank Macro Poverty Outlook database.

F. Inflation is measured monthly on a year-over-year basis. Sample includes 38 IDA countries. "Latest" refers to January 2024.

below overall growth in IDA countries and a 0.4 percentage point downgrade to the forecast from January 2024. Growth in IDA's small states, after picking up sharply in 2021-22 and moderating in 2023, is projected to slow further, from 4.5 percent in 2023 to 4.1 percent a year in 2024-25, broadly in line with the January 2024 forecast, as global tourism and travel stabilize at the prepandemic levels reached in early 2024 (UNWTO 2024).

Downgrades to growth forecasts since January 2024 have been concentrated in IDA FCS. Growth forecasts for 2024 have been revised downward in about 75 percent of IDA low-income countries and 60 percent of IDA FCS; in a number of cases, these downgrades have reflected delays in expected improvements to security and stability after increases in conflict and violence in 2023 and the first part of 2024.[2] The El Niño weather pattern that is prevailing in mid-2024 threatens to bring further damage to agricultural output, particularly in East Asia and the Pacific, Latin America and the Caribbean, and Sub-Saharan Africa (FAO 2023; World Bank 2024a).

Trade growth

Improvements in global trade growth are expected to support activity in IDA countries in the near term (figure 4.1.D). Global trade has shown tentative signs of firming in the first months of 2024 alongside the growth of industrial production (Kose and Mulabdic 2024). The contraction in global goods trade appears to have bottomed out, with volumes rising at the start of 2024. These developments are expected to support a modest pickup in trade growth as the services recovery tops out. Export growth in IDA countries is expected to edge upward as the recovery in global demand for goods gathers pace. Also, in some IDA countries, the pick-up in export growth reflects a recovery in the supply of key commodities as local conditions improve, production bottlenecks ease, and fertilizer prices fall. In some IDA FCS, a projected resumption of trade with neighboring countries factors significantly into the forecast.

Inflation

Inflation is expected to continue declining in IDA countries but to remain above its prepandemic average. Median headline inflation in these countries, on a year-over-year basis, has fallen from its July 2022 peak of almost 11 percent to about 5 percent in the first months of 2024 (figure 4.1.E). Nevertheless, of the 38 IDA countries that report consumer price indexes data monthly, 18 continued to

---

[2] In the forecast for 2024-25, notable performers include Guyana, Rwanda, and Senegal. Conversely, Haiti, Myanmar, and Sudan are expected to fare particularly poorly on account of ongoing conflicts and violence.

experience rising inflation in early 2024 (figure 4.1.F). About one-fifth of these 38 countries have double-digit inflation, in many cases owing to currency depreciation and elevated food prices. Despite the projected decline, inflation in IDA countries overall is expected to remain about 1.5 percentage points above its 2015-19 average over the next two years and about 1 percentage point above projected inflation in other emerging market and developing economies. Many households in IDA countries will continue to feel the effects of cumulative price increases, making it more difficult for them to recover the real income losses of recent years.

References

FAO (Food and Agriculture Organization of the United Nations). 2023. "El Niño: Anticipatory Action and Response Plan, August-December 2023. Mitigating the Expected Impacts of El Niño-Induced Climate Extremes on Agriculture and Food Security." FAO, Rome.

Kose, M. A., and A. Mulabdic. 2024. "Global Trade Has Nearly Flatlined." *Barron's*, February 21, 2024.

Macro Poverty Outlook database (["Poverty Data"]; accessed February 4, 2024). https://www.worldbank.org/en/publication/macro-poverty-outlook.

UNWTO (United Nations World Tourism Organization). 2024. *World Tourism Barometer and Statistical Annex, January 2024*: 1-49.

World Bank. 2024a. *Global Economic Prospects*. January. Washington, DC: World Bank.

World Bank. 2024b. *South Asia Development Update: Jobs for Resilience*. April. Washington, DC: World Bank.

World Bank. 2024c. *Africa's Pulse, No. 29, April 2024: Tackling Inequality to Revitalize Growth and Reduce Poverty in Africa*. Washington, DC: World Bank Group.

The pandemic-driven global recession of 2020 and subsequent crises inflicted large output losses on IDA countries, and these losses remain large. Over 2020-24, IDA countries are set to experience their weakest half decade of growth since the early 1990s. These developments have dealt a serious blow to IDA countries' progress on convergence of their income levels with those of advanced economies and on poverty reduction. Since 2020, per capita incomes in half of IDA countries have been growing more slowly than those of advanced economies—the largest such share since the start of this century. Weak growth prospects will make progress on poverty reduction in these countries more difficult. All told, this constitutes a historic reversal.

Output losses

IDA countries have suffered substantial losses in output relative to prepandemic trends. Output in IDA countries fell 4 percent below prepandemic trends in 2020; this gap had widened to 5.3 percent by 2023 and is projected to reach 5.7 percent in 2024 and 5.9 percent in 2025. Among IDA country groups, the steepest initial output losses in 2020, by far, occurred in small states, and these losses have been only partly recovered, with gaps relative to the prepandemic trend set to remain in double digits in percentage terms in 2024-25 (figure 5.1.A). IDA low-income countries (LICs) initially sustained smaller output losses relative to prepandemic trends that have since risen. IDA countries have suffered substantial cumulative output losses since the onset of the pandemic, especially IDA small states (figure 5.1.B). IDA countries facing fragile and conflict-affected situations (FCS) have also seen larger cumulative output losses than IDA countries overall, whereas losses have been more muted in LICs.

Growth

The recovery in IDA countries is projected to remain weaker than that in previous postrecession rebounds, including the recovery from the 2009 global recession, and also weaker than that in other emerging market and developing economies. Compounding effects of the unusual overlapping crises of recent years alongside longer-term scarring from the pandemic largely account for the weakness of the recovery from the 2020 global recession relative to earlier recoveries (figure 5.1.C). In turn, output in IDA countries is set to continue following a lower path than before 2020. These countries entered the pandemic-

FIGURE 5.1 Output losses and growth in IDA countries

Output in IDA countries has declined sharply from that in prepandemic trends. Output losses remain large, particularly for IDA small states. The recovery in IDA countries has been more muted than the equivalent after the 2008-09 global recession. Overall, IDA countries are set to experience their weakest half decade of growth since the early 1990s.

A. Deviation of output from prepandemic trends

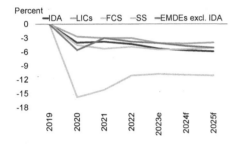

B. Cumulative output losses, 2020-25

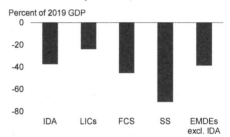

C. Expansions after 2009 and 2020

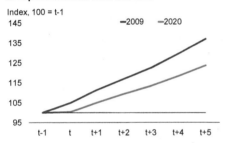

D. Annual average GDP growth

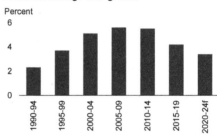

Source: World Bank.
Note: GDP aggregates are calculated using real U.S. dollar GDP weights at average 2010-19 prices and market exchange rates.
e = estimate; EMDEs = emerging market and developing economies; excl. = excluding; f = forecast; FCS = IDA countries classified as fragile and conflict-affected situations; GDP = gross domestic product; IDA = IDA countries; LICs = IDA countries classified as low-income countries; SS = IDA countries classified as small states.
A. Panel shows percent deviation between latest projections and forecasts from the January 2020 edition of the *Global Economic Prospects* report. For 2023 and beyond, the January 2020 baseline is extended using projected growth for 2022.
B. Panel shows output losses for subgroups of IDA countries over 2020-25 relative to prepandemic trend as a percentage of 2019 GDP. Prepandemic trend is based on January 2020 baseline extended using 2022 projections.
C. Indexes show the evolution of output in IDA countries around the global recessions of 2009 and 2020. *t* represents the year of the global recession.

induced global recession in 2020 more poorly prepared and with greater vulnerabilities than when they entered the global recession in 2009 (World Bank 2020). Weak health care systems, heavy reliance on tourism, greater debt vulnerabilities, exposure to financial disruptions, and high dependence on energy and other commodity exports—or some combination of these factors—exposed many IDA countries particularly heavily to the impact of the pandemic. Overall, in 2020-24, IDA countries are projected to experience their weakest half decade of growth since the early 1990s (figure 5.1.D).

The recovery from the global recession of 2020 is also expected to remain weak in terms of per capita income. Per capita income in IDA countries is projected to

TABLE 5.1 **GDP growth per capita**

	2010-19 average	2020	2021	2022	2023e	2024f	2025f
IDA	2.5	-1.8	2.4	2.0	1.5	2.1	2.3
IDA only	3.2	-1.4	2.3	2.5	2.1	2.9	3.1
IDA blend	1.8	-2.4	2.6	1.3	0.6	1.1	1.4
IDA low-income countries	1.7	-1.4	1.3	2.2	1.0	2.1	2.5
IDA middle-income countries	2.9	-1.9	2.8	1.9	1.5	2.0	2.4
IDA FCS	1.5	-4.0	-0.1	1.4	0.4	1.1	1.3
IDA small states	1.9	-13.9	4.5	6.5	3.0	2.5	2.6
Other aggregates							
Advanced economies [a]	1.5	-4.3	5.4	2.4	1.3	1.2	1.4
EMDEs [a]	3.8	-2.5	6.1	2.8	3.2	2.8	3.1
EMDEs excl. IDA countries	4.1	-2.3	6.7	3.2	3.7	3.2	3.5

Source: World Bank.
Note: Aggregate growth rates for IDA small states exclude Guyana. IDA sample includes 71 economies. "Middle-income countries" includes both lower-middle-income and upper-middle-income countries. e = estimate; excl. = excluding; f = forecast; FCS = fragile and conflict-affected situations; GDP = gross domestic product; IDA = International Development Association; IDA only = countries eligible only for IDA resources; IDA blend = countries eligible for both IDA and International Bank for Reconstruction and Development resources.
[a] The data presented for advanced economies and EMDEs reflect preliminary working assumptions and are subject to change. The World Bank Group publishes official forecasts for advanced economies and EMDEs only in January and June.

grow by an annual average of 1.2 percent over 2020-24, less than half its 2010-19 average annual growth rate of 2.5 percent (table 5.1). Some of the most vulnerable IDA countries are expected to fall further behind, with per capita income for 2024 projected to remain below its 2019 level in nearly one-third of IDA countries, including 42 percent of LICs and half of FCS (figure 5.2.A).

Convergence

The process of catching up with per capita incomes in advanced economies is expected to stall in IDA countries over the period from 2020 to 2024. Per capita income in IDA countries is expected to grow over 2020-24 at a rate (averaging 1.2 percent a year) almost identical to that in advanced economies, stalling the catch-up process in these countries. Indeed, over 2021-24, the period after the 2020 global recession, IDA countries are projected to experience lower average growth in per capita incomes than advanced economies, with earlier gains for IDA FCS slipping back notably (figure 5.2.B). The reversal is also broad-based: over 2020-24, average growth in per capita incomes is expected to trail that of advanced economies in half of IDA countries (figure 5.2.C).

This comes on the heels of slowing progress in IDA countries over the last two decades in closing these gaps (figure 5.2.D). In contrast, other emerging market and developing economies are expected to continue to catch up with advanced economies, albeit at a slower pace than the 2010-19 average, with per capita

FIGURE 5.2 **Per capita income growth in IDA countries**

Per capita income growth has been weak in absolute terms for IDA countries as well as in relation to that in advanced economies and other EMDEs. As a result, the process of catching up with advanced economy per capita incomes has stalled in many IDA countries.

A. Share of countries with lower GDP per capita in 2024 than in 2019

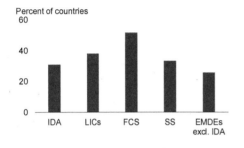

B. Annual change in growth in GDP per capita relative to that in advanced economies

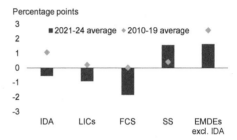

C. Share of countries with lower growth in GDP per capita than that in advanced economies

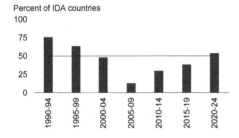

D. Change in growth in GDP per capita relative to that in advanced economies

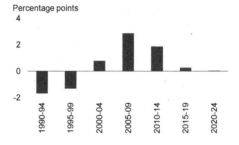

E. Cumulative change in growth in per capita income growth relative to advanced economies

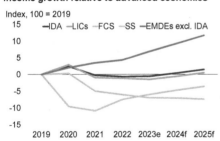

F. Per capita income in subgroups relative to that in advanced economies

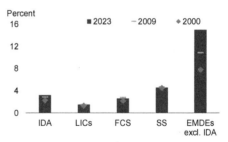

Source: World Bank.
Note: GDP aggregates are calculated using real U.S. dollar GDP weights at average 2010-19 prices and market exchange rates. Sample includes 71 IDA countries. e = estimate; EMDEs = emerging market and developing economies; excl. = excluding; FCS = IDA countries classified as fragile and conflict-affected situations; IDA = IDA countries; LICs = IDA countries classified as low-income countries; SS = IDA countries classified as small states.

FIGURE 5.3 **Extreme poverty in IDA countries**

The pandemic halted progress in reducing extreme poverty in IDA countries. Weak per capita income growth in many of these countries will constrain reductions in extreme poverty.

A. Share of population in extreme poverty, 1990-2030

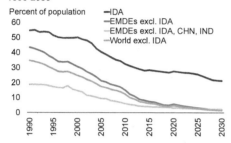

B. Extreme poverty in absolute terms, 1990-2030

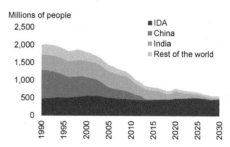

Sources: Mahler and Lakner (2022); World Bank, Poverty and Inequality Platform; World Bank.
Note: GDP aggregates are calculated using real U.S. dollar GDP weights at average 2010-19 prices and market exchange rates. CHN = China; EMDEs = emerging market and developing economies; excl. = excluding; GDP = gross domestic product; IDA = IDA countries; IND = India; LICs = IDA-countries classified as low-income countries; SS = IDA countries classified as small states.
A. Sample includes up to 75 IDA countries and 83 EMDEs excluding IDA countries. "World" includes 158 countries.
B. Sample includes up to 75 IDA countries. "Rest of the world" includes 81 countries.

income expected to grow more in other emerging market and developing economies than in IDA countries, as it has every year since 2021 (figures 5.2.E and 5.2.F).

Poverty

IDA countries' growth will remain insufficient to tackle key development challenges, with the pace of reduction in extreme poverty slowing and lagging established goals. Rates of extreme poverty declined globally over the three decades prior to the pandemic, with the decreases driven in large part by strong catch-up in China and India resulting from sustained high rates of growth in per capita incomes. However, the decline in poverty has slowed, both in IDA countries and elsewhere. Although the global rate of extreme poverty is expected to continue falling, it is expected to do so more slowly than in the decades before the pandemic. Consequently, the goal of reducing global poverty from its current level of about 9 percent to 3 percent of the world's population by 2030 appears out of reach (World Bank 2022). Moreover, extreme poverty is becoming increasingly concentrated, particularly in Sub-Saharan Africa and in FCS.[1]

---

[1] In Sub-Saharan Africa, which accounts for 52 percent of IDA countries, the share of the world's poor has grown, from 14 percent in 1990 to 62 percent in 2023.

The pandemic reversed about three years of progress in reducing extreme poverty in IDA countries. Extreme poverty—the number of people living in extreme poverty as a share of the total population—rose by 0.8 percentage point in these countries in 2020. Weaker prospects for growth in per capita incomes will make progress harder in the forecast period. Projected near-term growth will be insufficient to enable IDA countries to make major progress in reducing poverty (World Bank 2024).

Even if growth exceeds expectations, it is likely to pass through only in a relatively muted way to household consumption expenditures in many IDA countries, particularly those in Sub-Saharan Africa, stifling any potential boost to household welfare and poverty reduction (Wu et al. 2024). By 2030, an estimated 21.2 percent of the population in IDA countries will still be living in extreme poverty (figure 5.3.A). Although the average rate of extreme poverty in IDA countries is estimated to have returned to its 2019 level in 2022 and appears to have resumed a modest downward trend, key groups within IDA countries, including LICs, FCS, and small states, nonetheless had higher poverty rates in 2023 than in 2019.[2]

In absolute terms, more people are now living in extreme poverty in IDA countries than in 1990, and progress reducing this number over the remainder of the decade is expected to be modest. Globally, the number of people living in extreme poverty has declined sharply, from about 2.0 billion in 1990 to 691 million in 2023 (figure 5.3.B). China and India account for 1.1 billion of this reduction. In IDA countries, however, the number of people living in extreme poverty has remained stubbornly high. In 1990, an estimated 473 million people in IDA countries lived in extreme poverty; by 2023, this had risen to 498 million. This figure is projected to fall moderately by 2030, to 463 million. In the Middle East and North Africa region, however, extreme poverty is expected to increase over the same period.

References

Mahler, D. G., and C. Lakner. 2022. "The Impact of COVID-19 on Global Inequality and Poverty." Policy Research Working Paper 10198, World Bank, Washington, DC.

World Bank. 2020. *Global Economic Prospects.* June. Washington, DC: World Bank.

---

[2] Rates of extreme poverty increased from 42.1 to 42.6 percent between 2019 and 2023 in IDA LICs, from 34.2 to 35.2 percent in IDA FCS, and from 16.0 percent to 17.7 percent in IDA small states.

World Bank. 2022. *Poverty and Shared Prosperity: Correcting Course.* Washington, DC: World Bank.

World Bank. 2024. *Africa's Pulse, No. 29, April 2024: Tackling Inequality to Revitalize Growth and Reduce Poverty in Africa.* Washington, DC: World Bank Group.

Wu, H., A. Atamanov, T. Bundervoet, and P. Paci. 2024. "The Growth Elasticity of Poverty: Is Africa Any Different?" Policy Research Working Paper 10690, World Bank, Washington, DC.

CHAPTER 6
Risks to the Outlook

The economic distress of IDA countries would persist or worsen if the current weakness were to become more protracted or deteriorate further. Climate change could take a greater toll than currently expected, with changing weather patterns contributing to more frequent and more severe natural disasters, which would trigger large output losses and increase poverty. A further rise in conflict, local political instability, and violence could impede recoveries and exacerbate food insecurity in IDA countries. A range of external factors could adversely affect these countries and compound risks to their growth.

Risks

IDA countries are at risk of a lost decade of development. The overlapping crises of recent years have caused progress toward key development objectives in IDA countries to shudder to a halt, or even reverse. A more prolonged reversal in convergence of IDA country incomes with those in both advanced economies and EMDEs would have profound implications. With heightened vulnerabilities and limited buffers to respond, IDA countries are particularly exposed should key risks—many beyond their control—materialize. This could lead to further instability, increased fiscal pressures, and underinvestment, in turn undermining longer-term growth and development prospects. If these risks materialize, IDA countries could experience a lost decade in development.

Climate-change-related disasters loom large as a risk for IDA countries. Many IDA countries, particularly those located in tropical and subtropical areas, are exposed to climate-change-related risks.[1] Countries' limited fiscal capacity to respond to climate change and associated natural disasters, or their impacts on public sector balance sheets, could amplify their negative effects on growth (Milivojevic 2023). Natural disasters are likely to have uneven effects across populations, generally increasing poverty. Under an adverse scenario (combining a pessimistic baseline with large climate change impacts), more than 130 million

---

[1] IDA countries located in tropical and subtropical regions are prone to natural disasters such as hurricanes, typhoons, heavy monsoons, and droughts. In the Sahel region, countries like Chad, Mali, Niger, and Sudan endure arid climates, making them susceptible to desertification, with its adverse effects on agriculture and living conditions. Bangladesh and Pakistan experience seasonal river basin flooding, which, despite enriching soils, frequently results in extensive damage and displacement. Additionally, countries such as Bangladesh and Mozambique are at high risk from cyclones and rising sea levels.

people could be pushed into extreme poverty by 2030, many of them in IDA countries (Hallegatte and Rozenberg 2017; Jafino et al. 2020).

Worsening conflict and violence could undermine growth and impede development progress. Conflict has surged in IDA countries since 2023, notably in the Sahel region (figure 6.1.A).[2] Further escalation could intensify political instability, deepen food insecurity, divert scarce government resources away from growth-enhancing areas such as health and education, and undermine investment prospects. Weaker growth and development outcomes would result.

IDA countries are also exposed to an array of external risks. Many of these are not unique to IDA countries but would nevertheless have negative spillovers for them (World Bank 2024). The following risks are particularly salient:

- *Falling long-term global growth prospects.* The threat of weaker-than-expected long-term global growth compounds risks to the outlook for IDA countries. A longer-term perspective suggests that a more fundamental structural slowdown is likely to persist globally throughout the remainder of the decade. Potential growth is projected to fall globally to a three-decade low of 2.2 percent over the remainder of the 2020s—0.4 percentage point below the 2011-21 average and continuing a secular deceleration (figure 6.1.B; World Bank 2023a). The slowdown has multiple causes: the global labor force is aging and growing more slowly, and investment and total factor productivity are growing at weaker rates. A risk is that the decelerating trend could become more pronounced if, for example, labor market, education, or health outcomes fail to meet expectations; if investment falls short of projections; or if new recessions, climate disasters, or other shocks result in enduring damage.

- *Rising geopolitical risks.* Geopolitical risks increased sharply in the wake of the conflict in the Middle East that began in 2023, in addition to Russia's 2022 invasion of Ukraine (figure 6.1.C). Further escalations—especially if major oil producers become more embroiled—could significantly disrupt oil supplies and cause food and fuel prices to spike (Ha et al. 2023), with diverse but significant impacts on IDA countries. Geopolitical tensions could also prompt a flight to safety in international capital markets, resulting in currency depreciations for countries perceived as riskier, including many IDA countries, pushing up inflation and raising the costs of servicing

---

[2] Pervasive violence and political instability exacerbated the challenging economic and humanitarian situations in many IDA countries in 2023—especially those in the Sahel region—including Burkina Faso, Mali, Niger, Somalia, South Sudan, and Sudan, as well as in the Democratic Republic of Congo and Ethiopia.

FIGURE 6.1 **Risks for IDA countries**

IDA countries are exposed to a range of risks, including those involving conflict and violence as well as those related to trade and commodity market developments. The slowdown in potential global growth over the remainder of the decade will also present headwinds for growth prospects in these countries, especially when combined with geopolitical risks and the expected growth deceleration in China, a key economic partner for many IDA countries. The historically elevated real cost of external finance also threatens economic recovery.

A. Violent events in low-income countries

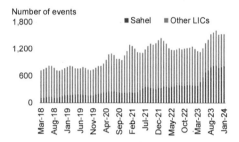

B. Potential growth

C. Geopolitical risk index and conflicts

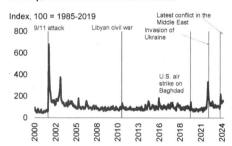

D. Exports to China

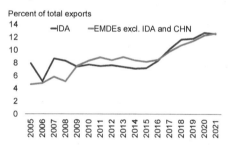

E. China's consumption of commodities

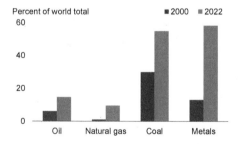

F. U.S. real interest rate cycle

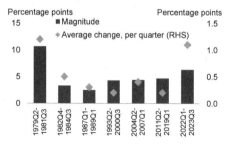

Sources: ACLED (database); Caldara and Iacoviello (2022); Energy Institute, *Statistical Review of World Energy*; Federal Reserve Bank of St. Louis; IDS database; Kose and Ohnsorge (2023); Refinitiv US, LLC; World Bank.

Note: AEs = advanced economies; CHN = China; EMDEs = emerging market and developing economies; excl. = excluding; IDA = IDA countries; LICs = low-income countries; RHS = right-hand scale.

B. Panel shows GDP-weighted averages of production-function-based estimates of potential growth for 29 advanced economies and 53 EMDEs, as in Kose and Ohnsorge (2023). Data for 2022-30 are forecasts.

C. Geopolitical risk index reflects an automated search of text of electronic articles from 10 newspapers on adverse geopolitical events. Last observation is February 26, 2024. Red vertical lines show adverse geopolitical events. Index is normalized to 100 throughout the 1985–2019 period.

D. Panel shows share of goods exports destined for China. Last observation is 2021.

F. "Magnitude" is trough-to-peak change and "Average change" is average change per quarter during periods of rising real rates. Real rate is U.S. policy rate minus one-year-ahead expected inflation from consumer surveys, adjusted for persistent errors.

external debt. Elevated geopolitical tensions and policy uncertainty could also dampen remittances, exacerbating financial challenges in IDA countries that rely on them (Chuku et al. 2023; World Bank 2023b, 2024).

- *A sharper-than-expected near-term slowdown in major economies, including China.* Such a slowdown could have severe consequences for IDA countries. China's importance as an export destination for, among other things, commodities, has grown in recent decades, particularly for IDA countries (figures 6.1.D and 6.1.E; Baffes and Nagle 2022). More than 12 percent of IDA countries' exports now go to China, according to recent data—a share that has risen by about half over the last decade. A more pronounced slowdown in China could also hurt IDA countries through shifts in global investor sentiment, financial conditions, and lending (Ahmed et al. 2019). China's position as a large creditor to many IDA countries indicates a further possible channel for adverse spillovers.

- *A protracted period of tighter global financial conditions.* A lengthy tightening in global financing would be challenging for IDA countries, as it would come on top of one of the sharpest and most synchronized monetary policy tightening cycles in recent decades (figure 6.1.F). A tightening of this type could be triggered by more persistent inflation, higher global interest rates (resulting from tighter monetary policies, pressures from fiscal deficits or strong demand), a rise in risk aversion, or a combination of any or all of these factors. Further depreciations of IDA countries' currencies as a result of higher global interest rates would raise inflation, drive up the costs of servicing foreign-currency-denominated debt, and likely be a drag on activity. As with other EMDEs, IDA countries with twin fiscal and current account deficits (76 percent of IDA countries as of 2023) would be particularly vulnerable to rapid capital outflows, which tend to accompany sudden increases in U.S. term premiums.

- *Increasing fragmentation of international trade and investment networks.* A rise in fragmentation along these lines could also complicate the outlook for IDA countries, even though they are often less integrated into global value chains than other EMDEs. The high concentration of exports in some IDA economies could leave them particularly exposed to sector-specific developments.

References

ACLED (Armed Conflict Location & Events Data) database (accessed February 1, 2024). https://acleddata.com/.

Ahmed, S., R. Correa, D. A. Dias, N. Gornemann, J. Hoek, A. Jain, E. Liu, and A. Wong. 2019. "Global Spillovers of a China Hard Landing." International Finance Discussion Paper 1260, Board of Governors of the Federal Reserve System, Washington, DC.

Baffes, J., and P. Nagle, eds. 2022. *Commodity Markets Outlook: Evolution, Challenges, and Policies.* Washington, DC: World Bank.

Caldara, D., and M. Iacoviello. 2022. "Measuring Geopolitical Risk." *American Economic Review* 112 (4): 1195-25.

Chuku, C., P. Samal, J. Saito, D. S. Hakura, M. Chamon, M. D. Cerisola, G. Chabert, and J. Zettelmeyer. 2023. "Are We Heading for Another Debt Crisis in Low-Income Countries? Debt Vulnerabilities: Today vs the pre-HIPC Era." IMF Working Paper 23/79, International Monetary Fund, Washington, DC.

Ha, J., M. A. Kose, F. Ohnsorge, and H. Yilmazkuday. 2023. "What Explains Global Inflation." Policy Research Working Paper 10648, World Bank, Washington, DC.

Hallegatte, S., and J. Rozenberg. 2017. "Climate Change through a Poverty Lens." *Nature Climate Change* 1: 250-56.

IDS (International Debt Statistics) database (accessed February 21, 2024). https://www.worldbank.org/en/programs/debt-statistics/ids.

Jafino, B. A., B. Walsh, J. Rozenberg, and S. Hallegatte. 2020. "Revised Estimates of the Impact of Climate Change on Extreme Poverty by 2030." Policy Research Working Paper 9417, World Bank. Washington, DC.

Kose, M. A., and F. Ohnsorge, eds. 2023. *Falling Long-Term Growth Prospects: Trends, Expectations, and Policies.* Washington, DC: World Bank.

Milivojevic, L. 2023. "Natural Disasters and Fiscal Drought." Policy Research Working Paper 10298, World Bank, Washington, DC.

World Bank. 2023a. *Global Economic Prospects.* June. Washington, DC: World Bank.

World Bank. 2023b. "Leveraging Diaspora Finances for Private Capital Mobilization." Migration and Development Brief 39, World Bank, Washington, DC.

World Bank. 2024. *Global Economic Prospects.* January. Washington, DC: World Bank.

CHAPTER 7
Natural Resources and Demographic Dividends

Natural resource endowments and demographic trends represent large potential sources of dividends for IDA countries. If effectively harnessed, these natural advantages could significantly enhance potential output growth, enabling IDA countries to achieve development goals more rapidly. However, the gains are not guaranteed, because they depend on the effective management of these endowments.

Natural resources

IDA countries boast substantial reserves of natural resources. These countries account for about 20 percent of global production of tin, copper, and gold (figure 7.1.A). Moreover, they hold pronounced shares of global production in certain agricultural sectors, especially tropical commodities. IDA countries contribute more than three-quarters of the global supply of cocoa, with Côte d'Ivoire alone contributing 45 percent to the global supply. These countries also account for about 17 percent of the global coffee supply, with globally significant producers including Ethiopia and Uganda.

Overall, IDA countries represent only a small fraction of the global supply of energy and most metals: 2-3 percent. Moreover, across energy, metals, and agriculture, specific commodity resources are often concentrated in a relatively small number of these countries. In some cases, including those of some IDA graduates, these natural endowments have been important sources of revenue and drivers of development over time. In others, however, the possesion of natural resources has arguably hindered development efforts, which indicates the importance of prudent and effective policies for resource management.

Several IDA countries have large reserves of minerals essential for the global energy transition. About a quarter of IDA countries possess critical mineral deposits (Andreonia and Avenyob 2023; Hendrix 2022; USGS 2024). Overall, these countries accounted for less than 3 percent of most critical mineral supplies on average in 2022, but there are important exceptions, such as cobalt, graphite, and rare earth oxides; a few IDA countries have a much higher share of global production of these minerals.[1] Apart from their shares in current global production, IDA countries account for large shares of global reserves of some of these commodities. New mining projects, however, have extended lead time, sometimes spanning decades, which underscores the strategic importance of IDA countries' mineral reserves.

Though the global energy transition will bring opportunities for IDA countries with resources critical to the transition, it will bring challenges for others. As the energy transition speeds up, the prospect of greater demand for minerals essential to it provides new opportunities for growth and transformation in IDA countries (Agnolucci et al., forthcoming; IEA 2022). However, deposits of some specific resources are concentrated in a small number of countries and can also bring pressures and risks to those countries that have them.

For IDA countries with endowments of critical resources, careful design and implementation of institutional and regulatory frameworks will be critical to ensure that the wealth these resources may provide is managed to support these countries' development objectives. These concentrations of resources also offer opportunities for specific IDA countries to integrate themselves into important global value chains. On the other hand, the same global energy transition will mean that several IDA countries that rely heavily on fossil-fuel exports will need to shift to low-carbon pathways. In some cases (such as Myanmar and Papua New Guinea), pivoting to metal production could help to reduce their dependence on fossil-fuel exports.

Many IDA countries also have natural advantages that could support solar energy production. Although it varies by geographic location, many IDA countries have high potential for long-term daily electricity production, both in absolute terms and relative to major emerging market and developing economies (EMDEs) (ESMAP 2020). For example, for about one-third of IDA countries, long-term daily photovoltaic power potential averages exceed 4.5 kilowatt-hours per installed kilowatt peak—a measure of the average daily energy produced by a solar panel system per unit of peak capacity. In contrast, Brazil, China, and India are assessed as having midrange potential (3.4 to 4.5 kilowatt-hours per installed kilowatt peak). As in other policy areas, infrastructure shortfalls, low institutional capacity, and scarce fiscal resources to fund projects involving solar energy mean

---

[1] The Democratic Republic of Congo and Myanmar, for instance, produce most of the world's cobalt. IDA countries contribute about one-fifth of global supplies of graphite, with Madagascar and Myanmar contributing 10 and 8 percent, respectively. Additionally, diverse mineral resources important for specific technologies provide opportunities for some IDA countries to increase their presence in global markets for critical minerals, such as silicon in Bhutan for solar panels, manganese in Côte d'Ivoire and Ghana for batteries, and tantalum in Burundi, Nigeria, and Rwanda for electronics.

FIGURE 7.1 **Demographic and resource dividends for IDA countries**

*Both natural resources and demographic trends represent potential dividends for IDA countries.
Although these countries theoretically have substantial solar energy output, their actual outputs are
below their current potential. IDA countries' working-age populations are projected to increase
notably by 2070. A 1 percentage point increase in the working-age population can boost GDP per
capita growth by 1-3 percent.*

A. Share in commodity production

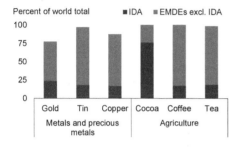

B. Solar power potential

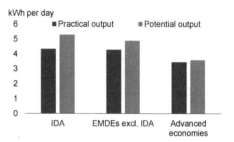

C. Working-age population

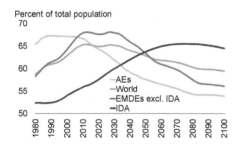

**D. Impact of increase in working-age population
on growth in GDP per capita**

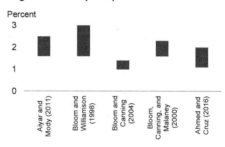

Sources: Energy Institute; Food and Agriculture Organization of the United Nations; International Cocoa Organization; Refinitiv US,
LLC; US Department of Agriculture; World Economic Forum; World Population Prospects database; World Bank.
Note: AEs = advanced economies; EMDEs = emerging market and developing economies; excl. = excluding; GDP = gross
domestic product; IDA = IDA countries.
A. "Share" denotes three-year averages during 2021-23 for precious metals, metals, and cocoa, 2022-24 for coffee, and 2019-21
for tea.
B. "Practical output" refers to practical photovoltaic (PV) output, which is defined as the PV power output of a PV system (specific
yield); in this panel, it is measured as the long-term power output produced by a utility-scale installation of monofacial modules
mounted in a fixed position at an optimum tilt, in kilowatt-hours per installed kilowatt peak per day; land with identifiable physical
obstacles to utility-scale PV plants is excluded from the measurement. "Potential output" refers to potential PV output, which is
defined as global horizontal irradiance, the long-term amount of solar resources available on a horizontal surface on Earth,
measured in kilowatt-hours per square meter per day; any land use constraints are disregarded. Data are from March 2020.
C. Panel shows population-weighted averages. "Working-age population" is defined as those ages 15 to 64.
D. Panel shows the impact on growth in GDP per capita of a 1 percentage point increase in the share of working-age population in
the total population. Study samples vary: Aiyar and Mody (2011) cover Indian states from 1961 to 2001; Bloom and Williamson
(1998) examine 78 countries between 1965 and 1990; Bloom and Canning (2004) analyze more than 70 countries from 1965 to
1995; Bloom, Canning, and Malaney (2000) focus on 70 countries from 1965 to 1990; and Ahmed and Cruz (2016) study 160
countries from 1960 to 2010. Bars show range of estimates.

that in IDA countries, practical output under current technology is about 20
percent lower than potential output (figure 7.1.B). However, with appropriate
policies, activation of this solar potential could enhance energy access and
resilience in IDA countries, in turn supporting further investment and growth
opportunities.

Many IDA countries also have significant economic potential via tourism. Tourism is already an important source of revenue for some IDA countries, particularly among IDA small states. It can be an engine for sustainable economic growth, through job creation, enhanced inclusion, and poverty reduction, among other things (IFC 2017; World Bank 2022). Promoting tourism, however, comes with risks related to resource depletion and environmental degradation. An overreliance on tourism can also make countries more vulnerable to global shocks, as was the case for many small states during the pandemic. A successful tourism-focused development strategy for a particular country is likely to be contingent on a stable political environment, strong institutions, solid infrastructure, and reliable health care provision—but these present challenges in many IDA countries. Nevertheless, benefits associated with tourism, such as deepening local value chains, enhanced human capital accumulation, and infrastructure investment, can become mutually reinforcing.

Demographic dividends

IDA countries can also reap substantial demographic dividends as the share of their populations who are of working age grows significantly over the next half century, while labor forces in most of the rest of the world decline (figure 7.1.C). This trend is already under way: IDA countries recorded an annual average of 32 births per thousand people during 2000-21, notably higher than the 19 births per thousand people observed in other EMDEs in the same period. Birth rates have been particularly elevated in IDA low-income countries and IDA countries facing fragile and conflict-affected situations. By contrast, working-age populations as a share of total population have been declining in the advanced economies for more than a decade. Working-age populations are projected to be stable in non-IDA EMDEs into the 2030s before falling.

The expected growth in working-age populations in IDA countries could have sizable economic impacts. A 1 percentage point rise in the share of a country's working-age population can enhance the growth of its per capita income by 1-3 percent (figure 7.1.D; Kose and Ohnsorge 2023). This is particularly true for Sub-Saharan African countries, where the demographic dividend, if combined with effective labor market reforms, could bolster growth significantly, adding an estimated 1.2 percentage points a year to potential growth between 2022 and 2030 (Kasyanenko et al. 2023).

Potential benefits and risks

Harnessing the dual potential of both natural resources and demographics is a complex task that offers significant benefits but also presents potential risks.

With comprehensive policy packages, supported by strategic investments, IDA countries with rich resource endowments, expanding working-age populations, or both can take advantage of them to accelerate development progress. However, realizing the opportunities offered by both will depend on implementing ambitious and well-designed policies geared toward delivering macroeconomic stability, boosting investment, enhancing human capital, creating more and better jobs, and overcoming substantial structural barriers to growth. Capitalizing on both advantages is a complex undertaking: a large literature stresses the risks as well as the opportunities (see, for example, Canning, Raja, and Yazbeck 2015). Without effective implementation of carefully designed and well-calibrated policies, including effective institutional and regulatory frameworks for the extractives sector, these potential advantages could instead become drags on development.

References

Agnolucci, P., V. Mercer-Blackman, P. O. Nagle, and H. Zahid. Forthcoming. "The Energy Transition: A Paradigm Shift for Commodity Markets." Policy Research Note, World Bank, Washington, DC.

Ahmed, S., and M. Cruz. 2016. "On the Impact of Demographic Change on Growth, Savings, and Poverty." Policy Research Working Paper 7805, World Bank, Washington, DC.

Aiyar, S., and A. Mody. 2011. "The Demographic Dividend: Evidence from the Indian States." IMF Working Paper 11/38, International Monetary Fund, Washington, DC.

Andreonia, A., and E. Avenyob. 2023. "Critical Minerals and Routes to Diversification in Africa: Linkages, Pulling Dynamics and Opportunities in Medium-High Tech Supply Chains." Background paper for 2023 edition of *Economic Development in Africa*, United Nations Conference on Trade and Development, Geneva.

Bloom, D. E., and D. Canning. 2004. "Global Demographic Change: Dimensions and Economic Significance." NBER Working Paper 10817, National Bureau of Economic Research, Cambridge, MA.

Bloom, D. E., D. Canning, and P. N. Malaney. 2000. "Population Dynamics and Economic Growth in Asia." *Population and Development Review* 26 (S): 257-90.

Bloom, D. E., and J. G. Williamson. 1998. "Demographic Transitions and Economic Miracles in Emerging Asia." *World Bank Economic Review* 12 (3): 419-55.

Canning, D., S. Raja, and A. S. Yazbeck. 2015. *Africa's Demographic Transition: Dividend or Disaster?* Washington, DC: World Bank.

ESMAP (Energy Sector Management Assistance Program). 2020. "Global Photovoltaic Power Potential by Country." World Bank, Washington, DC.

Hendrix, C. 2022. "Building Downstream Capacity for Critical Minerals in Africa: Challenges and Opportunities." PIIE Policy Brief 22-16, Peterson Institute for International Economics, Washington, DC.

IEA (International Energy Agency). 2022. *The Role of Critical Minerals in Clean Energy Transitions*. World Energy Outlook Special Report. Paris: International Energy Agency.

IFC (International Finance Corporation). 2017. "Women and Tourism: Designing for Inclusion." Tourism for Development Knowledge Series, International Finance Corporation, Washington, DC.

Kasyanenko, S., P. Kenworthy, S. Kilik Celik, F. U. Ruch, E. Vashakmadze, and C. Wheeler. 2023. "The Past and Future of Regional Potential Growth: Hopes, Fears, and Realities." Policy Research Working Paper 10368, World Bank, Washington DC.

Kose, M. A., and F. Ohnsorge, eds. 2023. *Falling Long-Term Growth Prospects: Trends, Expectations, and Policies.* Washington, DC: World Bank.

USGS (U.S. Geological Survey). 2024. *Mineral Commodity Summaries 2024.* Washington, DC: U.S. Department of the Interior.

World Bank. 2022. "Tourism and Competitiveness." Brief, World Bank, Washington, DC.

World Population Prospects database (accessed March 2, 2024). https://population.un.org/wpp/.

CHAPTER 8
Investment Needs and Policies

Increasing investment is a pivotal policy challenge for IDA countries, as they need to address substantial investment gaps to improve their growth prospects. History suggests that progress is possible.

Investment needs

To meet their development objectives, IDA countries have to address substantial investment needs. On a global scale, huge additional investments will be required to enable them to achieve the Sustainable Development Goals related to human and physical capital development while addressing climate-change-related risks (Aggarwal et al. 2024; Kharas and Bhattacharya 2023). Particularly in regions where extreme poverty is most severe, countries will require substantial investment to meet infrastructure-related development goals (Gill, Revenga, and Zeballos 2016; Vorisek and Yu 2020). In Sub-Saharan Africa, annual infrastructure investment needs surpass 9 percent of gross domestic product (GDP); in South Asia and the Middle East and North Africa, they are estimated at about 7.5 percent of GDP (figure 8.1.A; Rozenberg and Fay 2019).

Their significant infrastructure investment needs, both physical and digital, underscore the broader development hurdles confronting IDA countries (chapter 2). One-third of the population of IDA countries lacks electricity, and only 46 percent used the internet in 2021. Furthermore, only 31 percent of the population has access to basic sanitation facilities. Infrastructure shortfalls contribute to poor health and education outcomes. Despite strides since 2000, progress in addressing infrastructure challenges in IDA countries has lagged that of other emerging market and developing economies (EMDEs).

These investment gaps underline a critical, broad-reaching challenge facing IDA countries: the difficulty of marshaling the financial resources needed to meet their development objectives (Songwe and Aboneaaj 2023). Amid the overlapping crises of 2020-23, investment growth in IDA countries remained weak (as discussed in chapter 3; World Bank 2024a). At the same time, IDA countries' fiscal imbalances and debt-servicing costs rose significantly. The disparity between the urgent need for enhanced investment in infrastructure and human development, on the one hand, and the reality of subdued investment

FIGURE 8.1 Investment needs of and accelerations in IDA countries

Despite improvements, access to key physical and digital infrastructure continues to lag in IDA countries. These countries have large infrastructure investment needs that vary widely across different regions. They have experienced fewer investment accelerations than other EMDEs. These accelerations have often been transformative for EMDEs, including IDA graduates. Implementing a comprehensive package of policies raises the likelihood of investment accelerations considerably.

A. Infrastructure investment needs

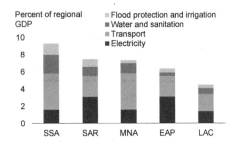

B. Probability of investment accelerations due to policy interventions

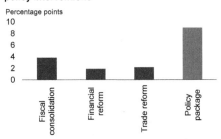

C. Number of investment accelerations

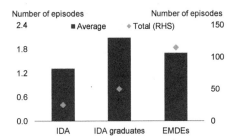

D. Investment growth during investment accelerations

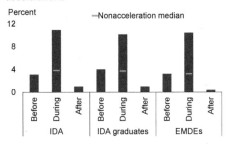

E. Growth during investment accelerations

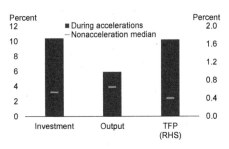

F. Growth in sectoral output before, during, and after investment accelerations

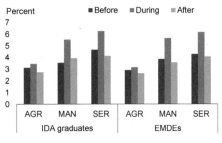

Sources: Dieppe (2021); Feenstra, Inklaar, and Timmer (2015); Rozenberg and Fay (2019); WDI database; World Bank (2024b).

Note: AGR = agriculture; EAP = East Asia and Pacific; ECA = Europe and Central Asia; EMDEs = emerging market and developing economies; GDP = gross domestic product; IDA = IDA countries; IDA graduates = countries that have graduated from eligibility to access IDA resources; LAC = Latin America and the Caribbean; MAN = manufacturing; MNA = Middle East and North Africa; RHS = right-hand scale; SAR = South Asia; SER = services; SSA = Sub-Saharan Africa; TFP = total factor productivity.

A. Panel shows average annual investment costs by sector and region for the preferred scenario, 2015-30 (Rozenberg and Fay 2019).

B. Panel shows result of a one-standard-deviation increase by means of policy reforms on the predicted probability of an investment acceleration; see World Bank (2024a).

C. Bars show the average number of investment accelerations per country over the period 1950-2022, whereas diamonds show the total number of episodes for each group between 1950 and 2022. Sample includes 19 IDA countries, 24 IDA graduates, and 69 EMDEs.

D.-F. Bars show the median growth rates of investment, output, and TFP, respectively, during accelerations in EMDEs. Sample includes 15 IDA countries, 24 (23 for panel F) IDA graduates, and 59 (56 for panel F) EMDEs that experienced an investment acceleration between 1950 and 2022.

D.F. At the 10 percent confidence level, differences between periods before, during, and after accelerations are statistically significant with the exception of the periods before and during an investment acceleration in the agriculture sector.

E. Orange bars show the median growth rates during all nonacceleration years.

growth and limited fiscal space, on the other, makes clear the hurdles that IDA countries face in seeking to achieve significant progress in addressing the challenges of development and climate change.

Policies driving progress

Nonetheless, history shows that IDA countries can make sustained progress in addressing these hurdles. Three dozen countries have successfully graduated from the IDA eligibility, 12 of them since 2000 (see table A.2). IDA graduates, ranging from the world's most populous countries to resource-rich economies and small states, have recorded some spectacular macroeconomic progress in recent decades. Several have become major players in the global economy, and per capita incomes in these countries grew strongly for extended periods, particularly in the decades before and after their graduations from IDA eligibility.

Large economies such as China, India, and the Republic of Korea successfully graduated from IDA eligiblity and are now important engines of the global economy. In both China and Korea, per capita GDP more than doubled in the decades prior to and after their graduations.[1] In China and India alone, the number of extreme poor has fallen by more than 1 billion since the 1990s (as discussed in chapter 5). Many IDA graduates now contribute to IDA as donors, with nine of them together accounting for almost one-tenth of net contributions in the last IDA replenishment round in 2022.

Countries have often graduated from IDA eligibility after they have undertaken comprehensive policies of reform to boost investment and growth. For instance, in Korea, which graduated from IDA eligibility in 1973, government policies (through strategic interventions and coordinated investment initiatives) enhanced returns on private capital, driving remarkable economic growth that began in the 1960s (Kim and Lau 1994; Rodrik 1995; World Bank 2024b).[2] Similarly, India's graduation in 2014 followed a prolonged period of robust

---

[1] World Bank (2015, 2018, and 2021) and Ferro and Nishio (2021) provide information about the cases of China, India, and Korea in the context of their IDA memberships. Korea joined the IDA in 1961 (with an annual per capita GDP of $1,063), graduated from IDA eligibility in 1973 (with an annual per capita GDP of $2,497), and as of 2023 had an annual GDP per capita of $33,788. China joined the World Bank and the IDA in 1980, with an annual per capita GDP of $421. It graduated from IDA eligibility in 2000 (with an annual per capita GDP of $2,142) and recorded an annual GDP per capita of $11,707 in 2023. India, meanwhile, had an annual per capita GDP of $294 in 1961 as IDA got under way; by its graduation in 2014, this had risen to $1,525, and as of 2023 it was $2,298. Korea is one of three IDA graduates now classified as a high-income country (along with Chile and St. Kitts).

[2] During the early 1960s, Korea possessed an exceptionally well-educated labor force compared with its physical capital endowment, leading to a notably high latent return on capital.

economic growth fueled by accelerated investment between 1994 and 1999 (World Bank 2024b). Policy reforms in the early 1990s targeted key economic distortions, strengthening the private sector and promoting international investment and trade (Ahluwalia 2002; Ahmad et al. 2018; Gupta et al. 2018). Overall, countries that have graduated from IDA eligibility have undertaken varied and multifaceted reform efforts, but many were able to change the structures of their economies in significant, lasting, and growth-enhancing ways.

Careful implementation of well-designed policy packages, tailored to country circumstances, is often key to the packages' durability and success. Particularly when capacity constraints and weak initial conditions prevail, the appropriate sequencing of reforms can be critical (IMF 2024; Kose et al. 2009). Political and social buy-in to reform agendas is vital to their success, particularly as the necessary reforms often entail short-term and sometimes concentrated costs in exchange for longer-term and more widely shared benefits. Clear communication and policy consistency are therefore important.

Countries should own their policy packages, which should be tailored to their particular circumstances. Successful packages often include fiscal and monetary interventions, as well as structural reforms, including strengthening macroeconomic policy frameworks, expanding cross-border trade and financial flows, and improving the quality of institutions. Although individual policy measures can help ignite investment accelerations—that is, sustained periods of rapid investment growth—comprehensive packages significantly increase the likelihood of sparking acceleration episodes (figure 8.1.B; World Bank 2024b). Since 1950, there have been, on average, about 2.1 investment accelerations in IDA graduates, but only about 1.3 in the current group of IDA countries (figure 8.1.C).

Investment accelerations have often transformed EMDEs, including IDA graduates. Investment grew at a median rate of slightly above 10 percent annually in a typical investment acceleration in EMDEs during 1950-2022, just over three times the 3.2 percent median growth rate in other years (figure 8.1.D). Output growth increased by 2 percentage points, and productivity growth quadrupled to 1.7 percent per year during accelerations (figure 8.1.E). Investment accelerations are also associated with higher growth in productivity through intersectoral resource shifts (Dieppe 2021; Hoyos, Libman, and Razmi 2021). During a typical investment acceleration, the composition of employment in a country shifts significantly away from the agriculture sector toward manufacturing and services, and output growth in manufacturing and services increases significantly (figure 8.1.F). Accelerations have also generally been accompanied by faster poverty reduction and convergence of incomes toward advanced economy levels, as well as increased access to infrastructure.[3]

The quality of investment is important as well, and it depends partly on strong governance and institutional frameworks. This is most directly evident in respect to public investment, in which reforms to tackle corruption and poor governance, as well as to improve the capacity of fiscal administration, are pivotal for improving investment efficiency (Chakraborty and Dabla-Norris 2011; Dabla-Norris et al. 2012). Countries that govern public investment projects better tend to register larger improvements in macroeconomic and fiscal outcomes (World Bank 2024b). The argument can be extended to private sector investment too: efficient and effective oversight is important for delivering stability and harnessing the benefits from investment.

References

Aggarwal, R., P. M. Carapella, T. Mogues, and J. C. Pico-Mejia. 2024. "Accounting for Climate Risks in Costing the Sustainable Development Goals." IMF Working Paper 24/49, International Monetary Fund, Washington, DC.

Ahluwalia, M. 2002. "Economic Reforms in India since 1991: Has Gradualism Worked?" *Journal of Economic Perspectives* 16 (3): 67-88.

Ahmad, J., F. Blum, P. Gupta, and D. Jain. 2018. "India's Growth Story." Policy Research Working Paper 8599, World Bank, Washington, DC.

Chakraborty, S. and E. Dabla-Norris. 2011. "The Quality of Public Investment." *B.E. Journal of Macroeconomics* 11 (1): 1-29.

Dabla-Norris, E., J. Brumby, A. Kyobe, Z. Mills, and C. Papageorgiou. 2012. "Investing in Public Investment: An Index of Public Investment Efficiency." *Journal of Economic Growth* 17 (March): 235-66.

Dieppe, A., ed. 2021. *Global Productivity: Trends, Drivers, and Policies.* Washington, DC: World Bank.

---

[3] These results collectively suggest a strong association between investment accelerations and improved macroeconomic and development outcomes. However, they do not imply a causal link. Indeed, there can be self-reinforcing dynamics between investment accelerations and other beneficial developments during these episodes. That said, the regular coincidence of investment accelerations and transformative phases of macroeconomic and developmental progress underscores the critical importance of periods of rapid and sustained investment growth (World Bank 2024b).

Feenstra, R. C., R. Inklaar, and M. P. Timmer. 2015. "The Next Generation of the Penn World Table." *American Economic Review* 105 (10): 3150-82.

Ferro, M. V., and A. Nishio. 2021. "From Aid Recipient to Donor: Korea's Inspirational Development Path." *East Asia & Pacific on the Rise* (blog), December 2, 2021.

Gill, I. S., A. L. Revenga, and C. Zeballos. 2016. "Grow, Invest, Insure: A Game Plan to End Extreme Poverty by 2030." Policy Research Working Paper 7892, World Bank, Washington, DC.

Gupta, P., F. Blum, D. Jain, S. John, S. Seth, and A. Singhi. 2018. *India Development Update: India's Growth Story.* Washington, DC: World Bank.

Hoyos, M., E. Libman, and A. Razmi. 2021. "The Structural Outcomes of Investment Surges." *Structural Change and Economic Dynamics* 58 (September): 245-55.

IMF (International Monetary Fund). 2024. "Macroeconomic Developments and Prospects in Low-Income Developing Countries—2024." IMF Policy Paper, International Monetary Fund, Washington, DC.

Kharas, H., and A. Bhattacharya. 2023. "The Trillion-Dollar Bank: Making IBRD Fit for Purpose in the 21st Century." Working Paper 181, Brookings Institution, Washington, DC.

Kim, J., and L. Lau. 1994. "The Sources of Economic Growth of the East Asian Newly Industrialized Countries." *Journal of the Japanese and International Economies* 8 (3): 235-71.

Kose, M. A., E. Prasad, K. Rogoff, and S. Wei. 2009. "Financial Globalization: A Reappraisal." *IMF Staff Papers* 56: 8-62.

Rodrik. D. 1995. "Getting Interventions Right: How South Korea and Taiwan Grew Rich." *Economic Policy* 10 (20): 53-107.

Rozenberg, J., and M. Fay, eds. 2019. *Beyond the Gap: How Countries Can Afford the Infrastructure They Need While Protecting the Planet.* Washington, DC: World Bank.

Songwe, V., and R. Aboneaaj. 2023. "An Ambitious IDA for a Decade of Crisis." Center for Global Development, Washington, DC.

Vorisek, D., and S. Yu. 2020. "Understanding the Cost of Achieving the Sustainable Development Goals." Policy Research Working Paper 9146, World Bank, Washington, DC.

WDI (World Development Indicators) database (accessed March 29, 2024). https://datatopics.worldbank.org/world-development-indicators/.

World Bank. 2015. *60 Years of Partnership: World Bank Group and Republic of Korea*. Washington, DC: World Bank Group.

World Bank. 2018. *IDA17 Retrospective: Maximizing Development Impact— Leveraging IDA to Meet Global Ambitions and Evolving Client Needs*. Washington, DC: World Bank.

World Bank. 2021. *At the Front Line: Reflections on the Bank's Work with China over Forty Years (1980-2020)*. Washington, DC: World Bank.

World Bank. 2024a. *Global Economic Prospects*. January. Washington, DC: World Bank.

World Bank. 2024b. "The Magic of Investment Accelerations." In *Global Economic Prospects*, January. Washington, DC: World Bank.

CHAPTER 9
Domestic Policy Priorities

Creating the conditions for investment accelerations and sustained improvements in longer-term growth in IDA countries hinges on success in implementing well-designed and comprehensive policy packages to foster stability, enhance resilience, and capitalize on these countries' advantages. Such policy packages should encompass fiscal, monetary, and external policies as well as deep-seated structural changes. The details and appropriate sequencing will depend on country-specific circumstances and characteristics. Particular attention should be given, however, to reforms to strengthen fiscal credibility and create policy space; improving frameworks and institutions (including those that support effective capitalization of natural resources); and improving education and health outcomes, which will also help leverage countries' demographic advantages. An overarching challenge for IDA policy makers is ensuring that reform packages are implemented in a sustainable and durable manner.

Fiscal policy

Markedly larger fiscal imbalances and greater debt vulnerabilities now confront IDA countries than before the pandemic. The multifaceted nature of the fiscal problems these countries face often necessitates comprehensive policy interventions. At the same time, the realities imposed by initial conditions and the impact of the overlapping crises of 2020-23 constrain these countries' space for maneuver (Ahmed and Songwe 2022). Fiscal policy thus has an important role to play in fostering macroeconomic stability, building resilience, capitalizing on the distinctive advantages of IDA countries, and creating the conditions for strong investment growth.

Building tax capacity is crucial to mobilizing additional domestic resources in IDA countries, which lags that in other countries. Tax revenues in IDA countries on average account for just 11.9 percent of gross domestic product, well below the 15 percent typically considered the minimum necessary to finance basic public services and development needs (see, for example, Gaspar, Jaramillo, and Wingender 2016). Increasing tax capacity can make it easier for countries to provide essential public services and build fiscal buffers (Doumbia and Lauridsen 2019). Stronger revenue collection can also increase the potential redistributive power of taxation and the financing available for social protection systems, thus facilitating poverty reduction (Lopez-Acevedo et al. 2023). Addressing informality in the economy and enhancing tax administration are two ways countries can increase revenues. However, they are often complex tasks for IDA countries, linked closely to institutional strength.[1]

IDA countries can make progress in addressing fiscal policy needs if the reforms they undertake are well designed. Reforms can focus on broadening tax bases, strengthening tax administration, and enhancing tax efficiencies (Okunogbe and Tourek 2023; World Bank 2023a). Shifts in incentives through the tax system can also play an important role, reinforcing complementary objectives. For example, eliminating fossil-fuel subsidies and introducing carbon taxes in tandem provide incentives for investment in energy-efficient technologies while also enhancing revenues (World Bank 2023b).

Enhancing expenditure efficiency and reallocating existing resources towards more growth-enhancing sectors and supporting the most vulnerable is critical. IDA countries generally have weaker spending efficiency in key areas than other country groups (figure 9.1.A). Progress in this regard hinges partly on strengthening institutional frameworks, because corruption and weaker law and order are associated with less efficient spending practices (World Bank 2023a). Countries should design social protection systems to help the most vulnerable, providing access to critical services and support.

There is also potential to cut less productive spending to facilitate more growth-enhancing or better-targeted programs. For instance, food and energy subsidies are extensive in low-income countries (LICs) but tend to be poorly targeted and fiscally costly (Coady, Flamini, and Sears 2015). Integrating subsidy reforms into broader reform campaigns, along with compensatory packages negotiated within societies, can help garner public support, especially by ensuring credible commitments to reinvest savings, as can employing communication strategies that focus on climate change mitigation, fairness, and efficiency in resource utilization (World Bank 2023b).

Strengthening fiscal credibility through improved fiscal discipline is also important. This can promote macroeconomic stabilization, paving the way for creating additional fiscal space and fortifying resilience against potential shocks. Commodity-exporting IDA countries—about 70 percent of the group—can particularly benefit from prudent fiscal policies, since excessive reliance on commodity revenues can leave countries' budgets vulnerable to commodity price volatility (figures 9.1.B and 9.1.C; Arroyo Marioli, Fatás, and Vasishtha 2023)

---

[1] For detailed discussions of policies to address informality, see Benitez et al. (2023); Mawejje and Sebudde (2019); Ohnsorge and Yu (2021); and Waseem (2018).

FIGURE 9.1 **Fiscal and monetary policy challenges in IDA countries**

IDA countries have lower public spending efficiency than other EMDEs. Revenues are more volatile in IDA countries, especially among commodity exporters, and fiscal institutions tend to be weaker. Most IDA countries operate some form of fixed exchange rate regime, and relatively few target inflation.

A. Public spending efficiency score

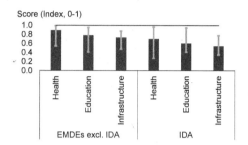

B. Resource revenues as a share of total fiscal revenues

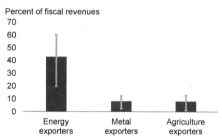

C. Fiscal policy volatility

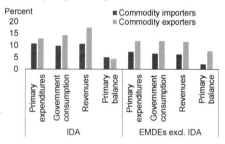

D. Fiscal policy procyclicality

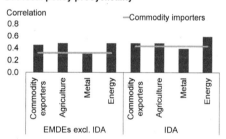

E. Fiscal institutions

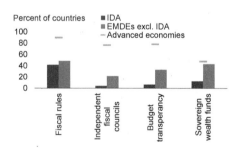

F. Fixed exchange rate and inflation-targeting regimes

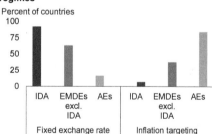

Sources: AREAER database; Arroyo Marioli, Fatás, and Vasishtha (2023); Arroyo Marioli and Vegh (2023); Davoodi et al. (2022); Herrera et al. (forthcoming); Fiscal Council Dataset; Fiscal Rules Dataset; International Budget Partnership, Open Budget Survey 2021; Kose et al. (2021); Kose et al. (2022); United Nations University World Institute for Development Economics Research; WEO database; World Bank.

Note: AEs = advanced economies; EMDEs = emerging market and developing economies; excl. = excluding; IDA = IDA countries.

A. Panel shows average efficiency scores for up to 69 IDA countries and 77 EMDEs excluding IDA countries over 2010-20 from Herrera et al. (forthcoming). Whiskers show minimum and maximum values. Horizontal line is the efficiency frontier.

B. Panel shows unweighted averages for 9 energy, 9 metals, and 10 agricultural commodity exporters, as of 2018. Whiskers show interquartile range.

C. Panel shows unweighted averages, by commodity group, of the standard deviation of the residuals obtained from regressing four dependent variables—real primary expenditure growth, real government consumption growth, real revenue growth, and change in primary balances (as percent of GDP)—on real GDP growth. Annual data over 1990-2021.

D. Bars show average correlation between the (Hodrick-Prescott-filtered) cyclical components of real GDP and real government spending within groups. Sample period is 1980-2020.

E. Panel shows, for fiscal rules and independent fiscal councils, sample of 75 IDA countries, 79 EMDEs excluding IDA countries, and 38 AEs; for budget transparency, sample of 47 IDA countries, 55 EMDEs excluding IDA countries, and 18 AEs; and for sovereign wealth funds, 74 IDA countries, 78 EMDEs excluding IDA countries, and 38 AEs.

F. Sample includes 75 IDA countries, 78 EMDEs excluding IDA countries, and 37 advanced economies. Inflation-targeting data are for 2021.

and their economies vulnerable to fiscal policy procyclicality (figure 9.1.D; Arroyo Marioli and Vegh 2023). Excessive reliance on commodity revenues can also bring on the "resource curse": a term coined to describe how commodity abundance, if not managed properly, can damage overall growth.[2]

Introducing and implementing fiscal frameworks and rules can enhance fiscal policy credibility. These frameworks can also improve fiscal policy outcomes if delivered effectively and in conjunction with transparency and stronger institutions.[3] However, IDA countries rarely have these frameworks in place, and their introduction has to take into account individual country circumstances and capacities (figure 9.1.E).

Monetary and financial sector policies

Containing inflation remains an important priority in IDA countries. Although average headline inflation has halved from its mid-2022 peak, it remains elevated, and countries have made uneven progress in reducing it, with price pressures persisting in many (see chapter 5). Recent signs of inflation remaining stubbornly high in advanced economies, and the possibility of global interest rates remaining higher for longer than previously expected, could also put pressure on IDA countries. IDA policy makers can indicate a readiness to tighten policies again should upward pressure on inflation, from currency depreciation or other factors, return. This may help contain any such pressures that do arise and to anchor medium-term inflation expectations (World Bank 2024).

IDA policy makers face significant challenges in maintaining credible monetary policy frameworks. A large majority of IDA countries operate with a fixed exchange rate or use the currency of another country (figure 9.1.F). These countries tend to give priority to exchange rate stability over monetary policy autonomy while counting on the credibility of the anchor currency's monetary authority to maintain low domestic inflation (Buffie, Airaudo, and Zanna 2018). Countries with more credible, transparent, and independent central banks, along with inflation-targeting monetary policy regimes, tend to experience better-anchored inflation expectations and smaller exchange rate pass-through from depreciation to inflation (Ha, Stocker, and Yilmazkuday 2020; Kose et al. 2019). IDA countries still have significant scope for progress in these areas, given that only a small fraction of them have independent central banks

---

[2] On the resource curse, see Bleaney and Halland (2009) and Sachs and Warner (1995) for detailed discussions.

[3] On these fiscal arrangements, see Beetsma et al. (2019), Caselli and Reynaud (2020), Gill et al. (2014), and Gootjes and de Haan (2022).

operating inflation-targeting regimes. However, for many IDA countries, this is an objective for the longer rather than the shorter or medium term.

IDA countries with some form of fixed exchange rate regime need to have monetary and fiscal policies consistent with maintaining adequate reserves and the credibility of the currency peg. This should help maintain price stability and anchor inflation expectations. More broadly, transparent communication by monetary authorities, combined with a clear and decisive commitment to central bank targets, can buttress the credibility of monetary policy frameworks, which would lessen long-term inflationary pressures (Ha, Kose, and Ohnsorge 2019). In addition, policy makers can act to conserve or replenish foreign currency reserves by, for example, demonstrating a commitment to policies that boost investor confidence and attract foreign capital.

Heightened volatility in global financial markets, should it materialize, could increase liquidity and solvency risks in IDA countries' financial sectors. In their banking sectors, currency and maturity mismatches between assets and liabilities need to be monitored. Emerging issues should be managed promptly, especially because of vulnerabilities—including in highly leveraged nonbank corporations, among others—to elevated interest rates (Koh and Yu 2020). Timely and transparent reporting of nonperforming loans is crucial for effective monitoring of banking sector health. Amid high debt vulnerabilities, the deeper public-private nexus in many IDA countries' financial sectors could make their banking systems and their economies more vulnerable to macroeconomic shocks.

Over the medium term, IDA countries could improve their frameworks for addressing potential banking sector stress. For example, they could refine their liquidity requirements to better address foreign currency liquidity risks and to ensure that assets deemed liquid are of sufficiently high quality (IMF 2023). At the same time, deeper domestic financial markets can help reduce risks relating to currency fluctuations and external financing flows and also promote financial inclusion; this needs to be balanced, however, with market oversight efforts (IMF 2024).

Structural policies

A wide range of structural policies can enhance the investment climate, promote investment growth, close development gaps, and help ensure that IDA countries effectively harness their relative advantages in demographics and natural resources. Indeed, structural policies are important for global poverty reduction efforts and sustainable development, not just for fostering growth (Wu et al. 2024). Priority areas will depend on country-specific circumstances, and the areas discussed in this section are not exhaustive. However, given IDA countries' capacity constraints, careful sequencing is vital to policy success. In many IDA countries, a focus on strengthening institutions and fostering human capital will be pivotal.

Improving health care and education provision is crucial to ensuring that favorable demographics in IDA countries can underpin economic gains. Increased working-age populations are helpful only if productive jobs are available and workers are well-equipped for them. Access to health care and education deteriorated during the pandemic, in IDA countries as well as elsewhere, and has been impeded since (World Bank 2023c). IDA countries suffered especially pronounced learning losses, with significant disruptions in South Asia and Latin America and the Caribbean (figure 9.2.A).

These setbacks could have a significant impact on growth and development in IDA countries, with projections pointing to a substantial reduction in future gross domestic product because of disrupted schooling, disproportionately affecting marginalized and economically vulnerable students (Azevedo et al. 2021). Conversely, improvements in health and education outcomes could help secure the dividend from IDA countries' favorable demographics during the coming decades, supporting inclusivity and bolstering potential growth. Concerted action to unwind the deterioration in education and health care and to enhance future prospects is therefore an important development priority.

Tackling the diverse challenges IDA countries face in regard to education will require comprehensive policies. Making investment in education a priority is pivotal for creating and maintaining a skilled labor force, for fostering innovation, and for fortifying social cohesion (World Bank 2018). Each additional year of schooling is estimated to increase an individual's hourly earnings by 9 percent (Psacharopoulos and Patrinos 2018), highlighting the value of bolstering education budgets.

Ensuring learning equality, with resources directed toward disadvantaged pupils, including those affected by conflict and displacement, is also important (Jin, Jirasavetakul, and Shang 2019). Countries should match training in vocational and technical skills to emerging economic needs. The focus on specific sectors will vary depending on country circumstances, but infrastructure (including that in relation to electricity provision and the energy transition), health care, agribusiness, and tourism may all be growth areas for many IDA countries.

FIGURE 9.2 Learning losses and gender gaps in IDA countries

IDA countries have suffered large learning losses from the pandemic, particularly those in which pandemic-related school closures were extensive. Despite a decrease in gender gaps over the past two decades, female-to-male labor force participation ratios in IDA countries have not increased comparably to those in advanced economies

A. Learning losses

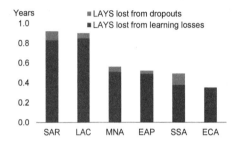

B. Female labor force participation

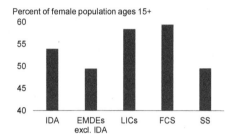

C. Female labor force participation, by region

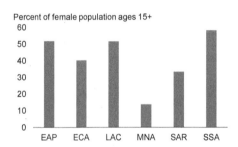

D. Difference in female-to-male labor force participation gaps between advanced economies and IDA countries

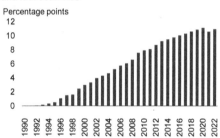

Sources: Gender Data Portal; Schady et al. (2023); WDI database; World Bank.
Note: EAP = East Asia and Pacific; ECA = Europe and Central Asia; EMDEs = emerging market and developing economies; excl. = excluding; IDA = IDA countries; LAC = Latin America and the Caribbean; LAYS = Learning-adjusted years of schooling; MNA = Middle East and North Africa; SAR = South Asia; SS = small states; SSA = Sub-Saharan Africa.
A. Panel shows the average lost LAYS by World Bank region, weighted by population. Regional averages exclude high-income countries. For each country, lost LAYS are calculated for each level of schooling and then averaged across levels, weighted by the duration of each level, as shown in Schady et al. (2023).
C. Panel shows IDA country subgroups. Data are modeled by the International Labour Organization for females ages 15 and older.
D. Panel shows unbalanced sample that includes up to 36 advanced economies and 75 IDA countries.

In the health sector, policy efforts should focus on accelerating the recovery of human capital while mitigating vulnerability and fostering resilience against future shocks. Notably, in IDA LICs, health care facilities face particular hurdles relating to water supply, sanitation, and hygiene services, in addition to waste management and environmental cleanliness (Hutton, Chase, and Kennedy-Walker 2024). Well-executed investments in comprehensive water supply, sanitation, and hygiene, coupled with effective health care waste management, can underpin substantial steps forward in these countries, through prevention of health-care-associated infections and enhancement of patient care, among other things.

Health and education in IDA countries can also benefit from a digital focus. Investments are needed to enhance the technological capacity and resilience of education, public health, and training systems. Embracing digitalization and fostering connectivity can boost the efficiency of countries' health and education spending while enhancing their resilience to future disruptions to health and education. Governments should also improve access to existing free and open-source education technologies, promoting inclusivity and equal opportunities, especially for marginalized students (Burns et al. 2019; International Commission on the Futures of Education 2020).

Closing the gender gap and taking other measures to increase labor force participation are essential as well. In IDA countries, about half of the female population participates in the labor force—slightly more than in other emerging market and developing economies (figure 9.2.B). This likely reflects the relatively large role of the agriculture sector in many IDA countries, especially IDA LICs. Nevertheless, female participation in the labor market varies widely across regions and is particularly low in IDA countries in the Middle East and North Africa as well as South Asia (figure 9.2.C). In addition, progress in closing gender gaps in IDA countries lags considerably behind that in advanced economies. In the 1990s, average female-to-male ratios of labor force participation were equal in IDA countries and advanced economies, but by 2022, participation was almost 11 percentage points higher in advanced economies (figure 9.2.D).

Barriers to female labor force participation such as skills mismatches, inadequate childcare, discrimination, and restrictive policies persist in many IDA countries. To overcome these problems, investments in education, social protection, childcare support, and legislative reforms are critical (Bussolo et al. 2022; World Bank 2022a). Simultaneously, IDA countries need to provide greater support for their youth to thrive. Active labor market programs and youth employment initiatives can help equip young people with the skills needed to access better job opportunities, ultimately fostering more inclusive economic growth (ILO 2023).

Well-calibrated measures to support the business environment can also be important for mobilizing private capital in IDA countries. In many cases, the private sector has a key role in filling investment gaps in these countries, including those in infrastructure (Lebrand, forthcoming). Liberalization in the areas of external financing, product market reforms, and trading arrangements can bolster growth in private investment, though the impacts vary depending on country circumstances. Strong and consistent government support, through effective implementation of regulations that promote the efficient and equitable working of competitive markets, among other measures, can play a critical role. Infrastructure-related incentives—for example, those to facilitate the energy transition—may also be required. Again, the success of measures will depend in part on institutional credibility.

Trade reforms and policies that strengthen and deepen countries' financial sectors, along with improved digital and technological infrastructure, can also promote investment growth in IDA countries. In many emerging market and developing economies, including IDA countries, reducing non-tariff barriers (for example, by shortening customs procedures, harmonizing inspection and labeling requirements, and improving trade-related infrastructure, including digital technology) can lower trade costs. Membership in trade agreements can integrate small and geographically isolated economies, a reality for many IDA countries, into global and regional value chains (World Bank 2020). For example, the African Continental Free Trade Area is a promising development in regional trade cooperation, benefiting many IDA countries on the African continent (Echandi, Maliszewska, and Steenbergen 2022). Increasing access to external sources of finance, by loosening the regulation of capital flows, promoting capital market development (for example, through improved contract enforcement and access to credit and local currency financing), and developing digital infrastructure to allow small firms and financial institutions to participate in financial markets, can also strengthen investment growth (United Nations Inter-agency Task Force on Financing for Development 2022; World Bank 2022b).

Underpinning these priorities, stability and resilience are often important to development progress but can also prove elusive. Stability and resilience matter in a purely economic sense, but they are also linked to societal stability and capacity to respond effectively to shocks. Fostering stability and resilience requires building institutional strength in the broadest sense, which remains a significant challenge for many IDA countries.

References

Ahmed, M., and V. Songwe. 2022. "An Economic Tsunami Is About to Hit the Poorest Countries: Inaction by the G20 Will Make It Worse." *Reliefweb* (blog), July 15, 2022.

AREAER (Annual Report on Exchange Arrangements and Exchange Restrictions) database (accessed February 10, 2024). https://www.elibrary-areaer.imf.org/Pages/Data.aspx.

Arroyo Marioli, F., A. Fatás, and G. Vasishtha. 2023. "Fiscal Policy Volatility and Growth in Emerging Markets and Developing Economies." Policy Research Working Paper 10409, World Bank, Washington, DC.

Arroyo Marioli, F., and C. A. Vegh. 2023. "Fiscal Procyclicality in Commodity Exporting Countries: How Much Does It Pour and Why?" NBER Working Paper 3143, National Bureau of Economic Research, Cambridge, MA.

Azevedo, J. P., F. H. Rogers, S. E. Ahlgren, M. H. Cloutier, B. Chakroun, C. Gwang-Chol, S. Mizunoya, et al. 2021. *The State of the Global Education Crisis: A Path to Recovery.* Washington, DC: World Bank Group.

Beetsma, R., X. Debrun, X. Fang, Y. Kim, V. Lledo, S. Mbaye, and X. Zang. 2019. "Independent Fiscal Councils: Recent Trends and Performance." *European Journal of Political Economy* 57 (March): 53-69.

Benitez, J. C., M. Mansour, M. Pecho, and C. Vellutini. 2023. "Building Tax Capacity in Developing Countries." Staff Discussion Note 23/006, International Monetary Fund, Washington, DC.

Bleaney, M., and H. Halland. 2009. "The Resource Curse and Fiscal Policy Volatility." Discussion Paper 09/09, Centre for Research in Economic Development and International Trade, University of Nottingham, Nottingham, UK.

Buffie, E. F., M. Airaudo, and L.-F. Zanna. 2018. "Inflation Targeting and Exchange Rate Management in Less Developed Countries." *Journal of International Money and Finance* 81 (March): 159-84.

Burns, M., M. Santally, Y. Rajabalee, R. Halkhoree, and R. Sungkur. 2019. "Information and Communications Technologies in Secondary Education in Sub-Saharan Africa: Policies, Practices, Trends and Recommendations." Background paper for *Secondary Education in Africa: Preparing Youth for the Future of Work.* Mastercard Foundation, Toronto.

Bussolo, M., J. A. Ezebuihe, A. M. Munoz Boudet, S. Poupakis, T. Rahman, and N. Sarma. 2022. "Social Norms and Gender Equality: A Descriptive Analysis for South Asia." Policy Research Working Paper 10142, World Bank, Washington, DC.

Caselli, F., and L. Reynaud. 2020. "Do Fiscal Rules Cause Better Fiscal Balances? A New Instrumental Variable Strategy." *European Journal of Political Economy* 63: 101873.

Coady, D., V. Flamini, and L. Sears. 2015. "The Unequal Benefits of Fuel Subsidies Revisited: Evidence for Developing Countries." IMF Working Paper 15/250, International Monetary Fund, Washington, DC.

Davoodi, H., P. Elger, A. Fotiou, D. Garcia-Macia, A. Lagerborg, R. Lam, and S. Pillai. 2022. "Fiscal Rules Dataset: 1985-2021." International Monetary Fund, Washington, DC.

Doumbia, D., and M. L. Lauridsen. 2019. "Closing the SDG Financing Gap—Trends and Data." Compass Note 73, World Bank, Washington, DC.

Echandi, R., M. Maliszewska, and V. Steenbergen. 2022. *Making the Most of the African Continental Free Trade Area*. Washington, DC: World Bank.

Fiscal Council Dataset (accessed February 17, 2024). https://www.imf.org/en/Data/Fiscal/fiscal-council-dataset.

Fiscal Rules Dataset, 1985-2021 (accessed February 17, 2024). https://www.imf.org/external/datamapper/FiscalRules/map/map.htm.

Gaspar, V., L. Jaramillo, and P. Wingender. 2016. "Tax Capacity and Growth: Is There a Tipping Point?" IMF Working Paper 16/243, International Monetary Fund, Washington, DC.

Gender Data Portal (accessed February 21, 2024). https://genderdata.worldbank.org/en/home.

Gill, I. S., I. Izvorski, W. van Eeghen, and D. De Rosa. 2014. *Diversified Development: Making the Most of Natural Resources in Eurasia*. Washington, DC, World Bank.

Gootjes, B., and J. de Haan. 2022. "Do Fiscal Rules Need Budget Transparency to Be Effective?" *European Journal of Political Economy* 75 (2): 102210.

Ha, J., M. A Kose, and F. Ohnsorge. 2019. *Inflation in Emerging and Developing Economies: Evolution, Drivers, and Policies*. Washington, DC: World Bank.

Ha, J., M. M. Stocker, and H. Yilmazkuday. 2020. "Inflation and Exchange Rate Pass-Through." *Journal of International Money and Finance* 105 (July): 102187.

Herrera, S., M. Massimo, J. N. D. Francois, H. Isaka, and H. Sahibzada. Forthcoming. "Global Database on Spending Efficiency." Democratic Republic of Congo-Public Finance Review, World Bank, Washington, DC.

Hutton, G., C. Chase, and R. J. Kennedy-Walker. 2024. "Costs of Health Care Associated Infections from Inadequate Water and Sanitation in Health Care Facilities in Eastern and Southern Africa." Policy Research Working Paper 10708, World Bank, Washington, DC.

ILO (International Labour Organization). 2023. *World Employment and Social Outlook: Trends 2023*. ILO Flagship Report. Geneva: International Labour Office.

IMF (International Monetary Fund). 2023. *Global Financial Stability Report: Financial and Climate Policies for High-Interest-Rate Era*. Washington, DC: International Monetary Fund. October.

IMF (International Monetary Fund). 2024. "Macroeconomic Developments and Prospects in Low-Income Developing Countries—2024." IMF Policy Paper, International Monetary Fund, Washington, DC.

International Commission on the Futures of Education. 2020. *Education in a Post-COVID World: Nine Ideas for Public Action*. Paris: United Nations Educational, Scientific, and Cultural Organization.

Jin, H., L.-B. F. Jirasavetakul, and B. Shang. 2019. "Improving the Efficiency and Equity of Public Education Spending: The Case of Moldova." IMF Working Paper 19/42, International Monetary Fund, Washington, DC.

Koh, W. C., and S. Yu. 2020. "A Decade after the 2009 Global Recession: Macroeconomic Developments." Policy Research Working Paper 9290, World Bank, Washington, DC.

Kose, M. A., S. Kurlat, F. Ohnsorge, and N. Sugawara. 2022. "A Cross-Country Database of Fiscal Space." *Journal of International Money and Finance* 128: 102682.

Kose, M. A., H. Matsuoka, U. Panizza, and D. Vorisek. 2019. "Inflation Expectations: Review and Evidence." Policy Research Working Paper 8785, World Bank, Washington, DC.

Kose, M. A., P. Nagle, F. Ohnsorge, and N. Sugawara. 2021. *Global Waves of Debt: Causes and Consequences*. Washington, DC: World Bank.

Lebrand, M. Forthcoming. "Policies to Support Private Investment." In *Promoting Investment Growth,* edited by A. Adarov. Washington, DC: World Bank.

Lopez-Acevedo, G., M. Ranzani, N. Sinha, and A. Elsheikhi. 2023. *Informality and Inclusive Growth in the Middle East and North Africa.* Middle East and North Africa Development Report. Washington, DC: World Bank.

Mawejje, J., and R. K. Sebudde. 2019. "Tax Revenue Potential and Effort: Worldwide Estimates Using a New Dataset." *Economic Analysis and Policy* 63 (September): 119-29.

Sachs, J. D., and A. M. Warner. 1995. "Natural Resource Abundance and Economic Growth." NBER Working Paper 5398, National Bureau of Economic Research, Cambridge, MA.

Ohnsorge, F., and S. Yu. 2021. *The Long Shadow of Informality: Challenges and Policies.* Washington, DC: World Bank.

Okunogbe, O., and G. Tourek. 2023. "How Can Lower-Income Countries Collect More Taxes?: The Role of Technology, Tax Agents, and Politics." Policy Research Working Paper 10655, World Bank, Washington, DC.

Psacharopoulos, G., and H. A. Patrinos. 2018. "Returns to Investment in Education: A Decennial Review of the Global Literature." *Education Economics* 26 (5): 445-58.

Waseem, M. 2018. "Taxes, Informality and Income Shifting: Evidence from a Recent Pakistani Tax Reform." *Journal of Public Economics* 157 (January): 41-77.

Schady, N., A. Holla, S. Sabarwal, J. Silva, and A. Y. Chang. 2023. *Collapse and Recovery: How the COVID-19 Pandemic Eroded Human Capital and What to Do about It.* Washington, DC: World Bank.

United Nations Inter-agency Task Force on Financing for Development. 2022. *Financing for Sustainable Development Report 2022: Bridging the Financial Divide.* New York: United Nations.

WDI (World Development Indicators) database (accessed March 29, 2024). https://datatopics.worldbank.org/world-development-indicators/.

WEO (World Economic Outlook) database, April 2018 (accessed February 17, 2024). https://www.imf.org/en/Publications/WEO/weo-database/2018/April.

WEO (World Economic Outlook) database, October 2023 (accessed February 17, 2024). https://imf.org/en/Publications/WEO/weo-database/2023/October.

World Bank. 2018. *World Development Report: Learning to Realize Education's Promise.* Washington, DC: World Bank.

World Bank. 2020. *The African Continental Free Trade Area: Economic and Distributional Effects.* Washington, DC: World Bank.

World Bank. 2022a. *South Asia Economic Focus: Reshaping Norms; A New Way Forward.* Washington, DC: World Bank.

World Bank. 2022b. "Update on World Bank Group Efforts to Facilitate Private Capital Investments." World Bank, Washington DC.

World Bank. 2023a. "Fiscal Policy Challenges in Low-Income Countries." In *Global Economic Prospects*, June. Washington, DC: World Bank.

World Bank. 2023b. *Building Public Support for Energy Subsidy Reforms: What Will It Take?* Washington, DC: World Bank.

World Bank. 2023c. *South Asia Development Update: Toward Faster, Cleaner Growth.* Washington, DC: World Bank.

World Bank. 2024. *Global Economic Prospects.* January. Washington, DC: World Bank.

Wu, H., A. Atamanov, T. Bundervoet, and P. Paci. 2024. "The Growth Elasticity of Poverty: Is Africa Any Different?" Policy Research Working Paper 10690, World Bank, Washington, DC.

CHAPTER 10
Global Support

Given the historic setbacks that IDA countries have suffered from overlapping crises since 2020—and the serious risk of protracted economic stagnation in these countries—the global community urgently needs to take action to advance progress toward IDA countries' development objectives. IDA countries are highly exposed to global shocks over which they have little control. They have limited policy room to enable them to effectively respond to these shocks. Concerted and sustained financial support from the global community is therefore needed to, among other things, help close the significant funding gaps that keep IDA countries from undertaking the requisite policies. Beyond financing support, redoubled global cooperation efforts are also needed to help these countries address challenges associated with elevated debt levels and climate change, to bolster trade and investment, and to support populations affected by food insecurity.

Financial support

Significant financial support from the global community has helped IDA countries make substantial economic progress in recent decades. However, sizable development gaps remain, and the additional pressures resulting from the pandemic and subsequent overlapping crises have contributed to slower progress or even reversals on some important metrics. Left unaddressed, these gaps could also hurt potential growth, exacerbating the current situation in IDA countries and leading to a lost decade in development.

Grants and concessional financing are imperative for IDA countries, but they are also important for global economic stability and prosperity. Any further slippages of development progress in these countries comes with a high probability of negative spillovers to other countries. Total grants to IDA countries have fallen by almost 30 percent in little more than a decade, even as grants from the IDA itself have increased (figure 10.1.A). Amid fiscal pressures intensified by the COVID-19 pandemic and subsequent crises, many IDA countries have largely lost access to international capital markets. Many have a pressing need for access to steady, predictable, and low-cost financial flows (Songwe and Aboneaaj 2023). Multilateral creditors have increasingly played a crucial role as lenders of last resort to these countries, and the countercyclical

FIGURE 10.1 **Global support for IDA countries**

IDA grants have increased significantly since 2016, yet overall grants as a percentage of gross national income have declined. Lower-income countries have contributed the least to climate change but have large needs for investment to achieve a resilient and low-carbon pathway. The composition of creditors to EMDE sovereigns has become more diverse over time. Trade-restricting measures have continued to grow, contributing to rising food insecurity.

A. Grants received by IDA countries

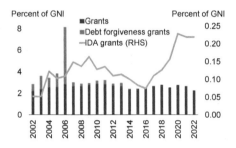

B. Annual investment needs for a resilient and low-carbon pathway, 2022-30

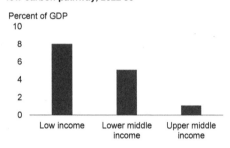

C. Composition of external debt, by creditor

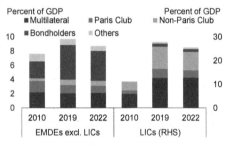

D. Policies to liberalize or restrict food exports

Sources: Global Trade Alert database; IDS database; World Bank (2022a, 2022b); World Bank.
Note: EMDEs = emerging market and developing economies; excl. = excluding; GDP = gross domestic product; GNI = gross national income; IDA = IDA countries; LICs = low-income countries; RHS = right-hand scale.
A. Grants are defined as legally binding commitments allocating specific funds for disbursement without any requirement for repayment. Technical cooperation grants are included. Data on debt forgiveness grants cover both debt canceled by agreement between debtor and creditor and reductions in the net present value of debt other than official development assistance achieved by concessional rescheduling or refinancing. Data are on a disbursement basis and cover flows from all bilateral and multilateral donors. "IDA grants" are net disbursements of grants from IDA.
B. Bars show estimates of the annual investment needed to build resilience to climate change and put countries on track to reduce emissions by 70 percent by 2050. Depending on data availability, estimates include investment needs related to transport, energy, water, urban adaptations, industry, and landscape.
C. Panel shows average of public and publicly guaranteed external debt weighted by U.S. dollar GDP. "Others" includes multiple lenders.
D. "Net number of policy changes implemented" is number of "liberalizing" changes minus number of "restrictive" changes. Export policies are those concerning export taxes, export bans, export licensing requirements, export quotas, and export-related nontariff measures. Data include changes relating to 33 three-figure United Nations central product classification codes pertaining to edible agricultural commodities and food items.

support they provide is pivotal for developmental stability and progress (World Bank 2023a).[1]

---

[1] In 2022, multilateral creditors injected a record $115 billion in new financing into developing countries, with the World Bank contributing nearly half of this (World Bank 2023a). Particularly for the poorest countries, multilateral creditors emerged as the primary source of new financing, through both concessional loans and grants (the World Bank's $6.1 billion in grants disbursed to IDA countries in 2022 was triple the amount provided in 2010).

Donors and multilateral development banks should continue to seek to catalyze financing in support of IDA countries' development efforts. This needs to complement IDA countries' own domestic efforts. The global community has an important role in fostering the mobilization of private capital for these countries through a range of financial instruments and support. These include credit enhancement, loan guarantees to address market failures, risk management (in relation to natural disasters as well as other risks), and liquidity solutions for local markets (G20 IEG 2023; World Bank 2024a; Zattler 2023). Such initiatives can help IDA countries address mismatches in investor risk appetites and investment offerings and tackle market failures and policy shortcomings. Donors and multilateral development banks can also help promote innovative investment products, such as environmentally focused blue and green bonds to support IDA lending for eligible projects. Technical assistance to improve IDA countries' capacity across a wide range of policy areas should complement these efforts.

Climate change

In addition to financial assistance, IDA countries need significant global support to address climate change. Transitioning toward a decarbonized global economy and preparing for the impacts of climate change via adaptation require substantial investments and financial resources. These will become more costly if delayed (World Bank 2022b, 2023b). The burden of climate change falls more heavily on poorer countries because weather-related disasters affect them disproportionately and they face wider existing gaps in development and infrastructure needs (Neunuebel 2023). Total annual investment needs—which include investments needed for a resilient and low-carbon pathway and for closing existing gaps in development and infrastructure—can be as high as 10 percent of gross domestic product in some IDA countries, with poorer countries facing particularly large gaps (figure 10.1.B; World Bank 2022c, 2023c).

Increasing IDA countries' access to financing to address climate change will require strong global cooperation. IDA countries as a group bear the least responsibility for the current threats arising from climate change, though they are heavily affected by them. In addition, climate change compounds existing fragilities in many of these countries. However, initiatives to strenghten their resilience to climate change—such as transitioning to climate-resilient agriculture (adaptation) or promoting renewable energy (mitigation)—face significant budgetary constraints. They have only small amounts of domestic resources, constrained fiscal and policy capacities for responding to disasters, and limited access to capital markets and private capital. International concessional climate finance—from the donor community and from private investors—will therefore be vital to address IDA countries' climate and development challenges and help them deliver on nationally determined contributions outlined in the Paris Agreement (IEA and IFC 2023; McCollum et al. 2018).

Debt restructuring and relief

To avoid the high economic costs of debt crises, the international community should act preemptively to reduce debt vulnerabilities in IDA countries. Without additional action, mounting debt-servicing costs and slow progress in debt restructuring could exacerbate the difficulties facing many of these countries. Debt restructuring and relief processes, particularly the Group of Twenty Common Framework, require improvements to address the sovereign debt challenges of the 2020s: they have delivered debt relief too slowly and are ill equipped to manage the much more diverse landscape of private and official creditors that has emerged in recent times (figure 10.1.C; Chuku et al. 2023; Gill 2022; World Bank 2024b). Measures that enhance debt transparency, which help contain debt-related vulnerabilities, restore fiscal space, and encourage external financing, can complement debt restructuring and relief efforts (World Bank 2023b). Greater concessional lending, earlier access to concessional financing, and more grants are also needed to support IDA countries in delivering growth-enhancing investments while containing debt-related risks.

Trade fragmentation and food insecurity

Boosting international trade and averting fragmentation of trade and investment networks are key global priorities that also matter for IDA countries. Disruptions to global value chains, whether from geopolitical conflict or trade policy restrictions, can lead to significant welfare losses globally, with particular harm to developing economies. Trade fragmentation can exacerbate food insecurity: many IDA countries rely heavily on food imports and are thus vulnerable to fluctuations in international food prices (Laborde, Lakatos, and Martin 2019). Since the onset of the pandemic, however, the number of new policies restricting food exports has far exceeded that of those aimed at liberalizing them (figure 10.1.D).

To address these challenges confronting IDA countries, it is imperative to bolster the resilience of the trading system to shocks, including those stemming from intensifying geopolitical tensions. This underscores the urgent need for stronger international cooperation. Enhancing food systems' resilience requires collective action (Voegele 2022). Furthermore, the global community must redouble its efforts to assist IDA countries in diversifying their products and markets and enhancing their access to trade finance, especially for the most vulnerable countries.

References

Chuku, C., P. Samal, J. Saito, D. S. Hakura, M. Chamon, M. D. Cerisola, G. Chabert, and J. Zettelmeyer. 2023. "Are We Heading for Another Debt Crisis in Low-Income Countries? Debt Vulnerabilities: Today vs the pre-HIPC Era." IMF Working Paper 23/79, International Monetary Fund, Washington, DC.

G20 IEG (Group of Twenty Independent Experts Group). 2023. *The Triple Agenda: A Roadmap for Better, Bolder, and Bigger MDBs.* Report of the Independent Expert Group. New Delhi: G20.

Gill, I. S. 2022. "It's Time to End the Slow-Motion Tragedy in Debt Restructurings." *Brookings Institution Commentary* (blog), February 25, 2022.

Global Trade Alert database (accessed February 4, 2024). https://www.globaltradealert.org/global_dynamics.

IDS (International Debt Statistics) database (accessed February 21, 2024). https://www.worldbank.org/en/programs/debt-statistics/ids.

IEA (International Energy Agency) and IFC (International Finance Corporation). 2023. "Scaling Up Private Finance for Clean Energy in Emerging and Developing Economies." International Finance Corporation, Washington DC.

Laborde, D., C. Lakatos, and W. Martin. 2019. "Poverty Impacts of Food Price Shocks and Policies." In *Inflation in Emerging and Developing Economies: Evolution, Drivers, and Policies*, edited by J. Ha, M. A. Kose, and F. Ohnsorge, 371-99. Washington, DC: World Bank.

McCollum, D. L., W. Zhou, C. Bertram, H. S. De Boer, V. Bosetti, S. Busch, J. Despres, et al. 2018. "Energy Investment Needs for Fulfilling the Paris Agreement and Achieving the Sustainable Development Goals." *Nature Energy* 3 (7): 589-99.

Neunuebel, C. 2023. "What the World Bank's Country Climate and Development Reports Tell Us about the Debt-Climate Nexus in Low-Income Countries." World Resources Institute, Washington, DC.

Songwe, V., and R. Aboneaaj. 2023. "An Ambitious IDA for a Decade of Crisis." Center for Global Development, Washington, DC.

Voegele, J. 2022. "How to Manage the World's Fertilizers to Avoid a Prolonged Food Crisis." *World Bank Voices* (blog), July 22, 2022.

World Bank. 2022a. *Global Economic Prospects.* June. Washington, DC: World Bank.

World Bank. 2022b. "Climate and Development: An Agenda for Action." Emerging Insights from World Bank Group 2021-22 Country Climate Development Reports, World Bank, Washington, DC.

World Bank. 2022c. "Update on World Bank Group Efforts to Facilitate Private Capital Investments." World Bank, Washington DC.

World Bank. 2023a. *International Debt Statistics Report.* Washington, DC: World Bank.

World Bank. 2023b. *South Asia Development Update: Toward Faster, Cleaner Growth.* Washington, DC: World Bank.

World Bank. 2023c. "The Development, Climate, and Nature Crisis: Solutions to End Poverty on a Livable Planet." World Bank, Washington, DC.

World Bank. 2024a. "The Magic of Investment Accelerations." In *Global Economic Prospects*, January. Washington, DC: World Bank.

World Bank. 2024b. *Global Economic Prospects.* January. Washington, DC: World Bank.

Zattler, J. 2023. "The Annual Meetings: Time to Walk the Talk on Private Sector Mobilisation for Climate." *Center for Global Development* (blog), October 10, 2023.

CHAPTER 11
Conclusion

IDA countries face an array of persistent development challenges that the COVID-19 pandemic and subsequent crises have exacerbated. They have recovered from the pandemic-induced global recession only weakly relative to their rebound from the 2008-09 global recession, as well as to other emerging market and developing economies and to advanced economies, in terms of per capita income growth as well as other measures. This subdued growth has substantially hindered their progress toward global development objectives. Advances in reducing extreme poverty in these countries, for example, have stalled after years of hard-fought progress. Debt vulnerabilities and mounting debt-servicing costs further darken the outlook for IDA countries. Food insecurity in these countries has surged. The income gap between many IDA countries and the rest of the world looks set to widen even further. This constitutes a historic reversal in development.

The current cohort of IDA countries is facing an exceptional confluence of circumstances, but country specifics also matter. Conventional policy packages that worked in the cases of previous success stories may not be sufficient or viable to address the binding constraints facing some current IDA countries. Climate-related vulnerabilities pose growing challenges for these countries, and broader measures beyond economic policy reforms may be necessary to foster stability for those in situations affected by persistent fragility and conflict.

Urgent action is needed to avoid further deterioration, accelerate progress, and chart a course toward a more hopeful future. Despite the multitude of challenges confronting IDA countries, they have significant agency to drive transformative change. The priority should be creating the conditions required to support stronger investment growth. Bringing these conditions about (via fiscal, health, and educational advances as well as strengthened institutions, among other measures) and delivering investment accelerations can help support these countries' income growth, drive poverty reduction among their populations, and address their infrastructure gaps.

Putting in place required policy packages may be a daunting prospect, but these policy packages are vital for investment and sustainable growth. Optimal interventions and their sequencing will differ from country to country, but key actions often include enacting fiscal reforms to strengthen discipline and contain deficits, enhancing the credibility of fiscal policy, and creating space for investment. Stronger governance and institutional frameworks are crucial here. Moreover, they are important for boosting resilience and ensuring that IDA countries' natural resource endowments bring lasting benefits. Education and health care improvements are also critical, for capitalizing on demographic advantages, among other things; they also support more and better jobs. Global support is also pivotal, both to directly assist IDA countries in delivering in these areas and to address global challenges that, left unchecked, will have a disproportionate impact on their economies. Private investment has an important role, but so too does public support, including from the international community as well as others. In some cases, parallel reforms to provide durable support for societal stability will be key.

Without comprehensive domestic policy interventions—and global support—development objectives in IDA countries will fall further out of reach. Despite efforts by many of these countries to improve their prospects, they have suffered significant and adverse spillovers from external conditions and global shocks. These factors have impeded their development progress and macroeconomic reform efforts. Escalating debt-servicing costs leave little room for IDA countries to expedite the investment agenda in the short term, potentially compelling many to reduce essential expenditures on education, health, and infrastructure, often from low base levels. This situation not only jeopardizes their immediate development but also risks erosions to their long-term growth prospects, putting agreed-upon development objectives even further out of reach.

A brighter future is possible for IDA countries, however. Through strategic policy making and concerted efforts, they can chart a course toward long-term shared prosperity, inclusive growth, and greater resilience in the face of adversity. History offers many examples of former IDA countries implementing successful policy packages, accelerating investment, and achieving significant development progress. Although current IDA countries face major obstacles, their demographic profiles and resource wealth also offer several comparative advantages that, if harnessed effectively, could support their own development and advance global objectives too.

A constructive approach to addressing the obstacles facing IDA countries in seeking this brighter future must involve much greater global support and cooperation. This is especially important because private financing and concessional lending to IDA countries have declined in recent years.

Collaborative efforts and sustained, stable, well-targeted support are crucial to driving meaningful change and advancing the collective prosperity of these countries and the global community alike. Enhanced international cooperation is also required to tackle the threats climate change poses, again both for these countries and for the world more broadly. In addition, the global community needs to guard against the fragmentation of trade and investment networks, by making it a priority to put a rules-based international trading system in place and by expanding trade agreements, as well as by taking other appropriate measures. Global cooperation is also critical to address the pressing issues of mounting food insecurity and conflict. Progress across all these measures is imperative for giving IDA countries the best possible chance of unwinding the reversals they have experienced, breaking free from their current bleak trajectory, and embarking on a brighter development path.

TABLE A.1 Characteristics of IDA countries

Countries	IDA only	IDA blend	Low-income countries	Agriculture exporters	Commodity exporters	Metal exporters	Oil exporters	Energy exporters	Small states	FCS	Tourism reliant
	60	15	25	28	52	17	10	11	24	33	15
Afghanistan	X		X							X	
Bangladesh	X										
Benin	X			X	X						
Bhutan	X				X	X		X	X		
Burkina Faso	X		X		X	X				X	
Burundi	X		X	X	X					X	
Cabo Verde		X		X	X				X		X
Cambodia	X			X	X						X
Cameroon		X			X		X	X		X	
Central African Republic	X		X	X	X	X		X		X	
Chad	X		X	X	X		X	X		X	
Comoros	X			X	X				X	X	
Congo, Dem. Rep.	X		X		X	X				X	
Congo, Rep.		X			X		X	X		X	
Côte d'Ivoire	X			X	X						
Djibouti	X								X		
Dominica		X							X		X
Eritrea	X		X		X	X				X	
Ethiopia	X		X	X	X					X	
Fiji		X		X	X				X		X
Gambia, The	X		X	X	X				X		
Ghana	X				X		X	X			
Grenada		X							X		X

TABLE A.1 Characteristics of IDA countries (continued)

Countries	IDA only	IDA blend	Low-income countries	Agriculture exporters	Commodity exporters	Metal exporters	Oil exporters	Energy exporters	Small states	FCS	Tourism reliant
	60	15	25	28	52	17	10	11	24	33	15
Guinea	X				X	X					
Guinea-Bissau	X		X	X	X				X	X	
Guyana	X				X		X	X	X		
Haiti	X									X	
Honduras	X			X	X						
Kenya		X		X	X						
Kiribati	X								X	X	
Kosovo	X				X	X				X	
Kyrgyz Republic	X				X	X					
Lao PDR	X			X	X						
Lesotho	X								X		
Liberia	X		X	X	X	X				X	
Madagascar	X		X	X	X						
Malawi	X		X	X	X						
Maldives	X								X		X
Mali	X		X	X	X					X	
Marshall Islands	X								X	X	X
Mauritania	X				X	X				X	
Micronesia, Fed. Sts.	X								X	X	X
Mozambique	X		X		X	X				X	
Myanmar	X			X	X		X	X		X	
Nepal	X										
Nicaragua	X			X	X						
Niger	X		X		X	X	X	X		X	
Nigeria		X			X		X	X		X	

TABLE A.1 Characteristics of IDA countries (continued)

Countries	IDA only	IDA blend	Low-income countries	Agriculture exporters	Commodity exporters	Metal exporters	Oil exporters	Energy exporters	Small states	FCS	Tourism reliant
	60	15	25	28	52	17	10	11	24	33	15
Pakistan		X									
Papua New Guinea		X			X	X				X	
Rwanda	X		X	X	X						
Samoa	X								X		X
São Tomé and Príncipe	X			X	X				X	X	
Senegal	X			X	X						
Sierra Leone	X		X		X	X					
Solomon Islands	X			X	X				X	X	
Somalia	X		X							X	
South Sudan	X		X		X		X	X		X	
Sri Lanka	X										
St. Lucia		X							X		X
St. Vincent and the Grenadines		X							X		X
Sudan	X		X	X	X	X				X	
Syrian Arab Republic	X		X							X	
Tajikistan	X			X	X	X					
Tanzania	X			X	X						
Timor-Leste		X			X		X	X	X	X	
Togo	X		X	X	X						
Tonga	X								X		X
Tuvalu	X								X	X	
Uganda	X		X	X	X						
Uzbekistan		X		X	X						

TABLE A.1 Characteristics of IDA countries (*continued*)

Countries	IDA only	IDA blend	Low-income countries	Agriculture exporters	Commodity exporters	Metal exporters	Oil exporters	Energy exporters	Small states	FCS	Tourism reliant
	60	15	25	28	52	17	10	11	24	33	15
Vanuatu	X								X		X
Yemen, Rep.	X		X		X		X	X		X	
Zambia	X				X	X					
Zimbabwe		X		X	X					X	

Sources: UN World Tourism Organization; World Bank.

Note: Tourism-reliant countries are those with inbound tourism expenditure as a share of GDP during 2015-19 above the 3rd quartile of the share in all EMDEs, based on UN World Tourism Organization data. Agriculture-exporting and energy-exporting economies are those where exports of agriculture or energy commodities accounted for 20 percent or more of total exports, on average, in 2017-19. Economies that meet these thresholds as a result of reexports are excluded. FCS = fragile and conflict-affected situations; IDA only = countries eligible only for IDA resources; IDA blend = countries eligible for both IDA and International Bank for Reconstruction and Development resources.

TABLE A.2 **IDA graduates**

IDA graduate	Fiscal year of last IDA credit on initial graduation	"Reverse graduation": year of reentry	Notes
Albania	FY08		
Angola	FY14		
Armenia	FY14		
Azerbaijan	FY11		
Bolivia	FY17		
Bosnia and Herzegovina	FY14		
Botswana	FY74		
Cameroon	FY81	FY94	
Chile	FY61		High-income country
China	FY99		
Colombia	FY62		
Congo, Rep.	FY82	FY94	
Costa Rica	FY62		
Côte D'Ivoire	FY73	FY92	
Dominican Republic	FY73		
Ecuador	FY74		
Egypt	FY81; FY99	FY91	Reentered FY91; graduated again FY99
El Salvador	FY77		
Equatorial Guinea	FY93		Remained eligible until graduating from IDA in FY99
Eswatini	FY75		
Georgia	FY14		
Honduras	FY80		
India	FY14		
Indonesia	FY80; FY08	FY99	Reentered FY99; graduated again FY08
Jordan	FY78		
Korea, Rep.	FY73		High-income country
Mauritius	FY75		
Moldova	FY20		
Mongolia	FY20		
Montenegro	FY08		Graduated from the IDA as of July 6, 2007 (date of approval of the last IDA credit—delay from FY07)
Morocco	FY75		
Nicaragua	FY81	FY91	
Nigeria	FY65	FY89	
North Macedonia	FY02		
Papua New Guinea	FY83	FY03	Became blend country in 2003

TABLE A.2 IDA graduates (*continued*)

IDA graduate	Fiscal year of last IDA credit on initial graduation	"Reverse graduation": year of reentry	Notes
Paraguay	FY77		
Philippines	FY79; FY93	FY91	Reentered FY91; graduated again FY93
Serbia	FY08		
Sri Lanka	FY17	FY23	
St. Kitts	FY94		High-income country
Syrian Arab Republic	FY74	FY17	
Thailand	FY79		
Tunisia	FY79		
Türkiye	FY73		
Vietnam	FY17		
Zimbabwe	FY83	FY92	

Sources: International Development Association; World Bank.

Note: Table shows, for each IDA country listed, the IDA fiscal year (FY) in which the country graduated from IDA eligibility and, for those that reentered, the year they did so. IDA fiscal years run from July to June. In total, 36 countries have graduated from the IDA: their graduations from IDA remain effective. The 10 countries that have "reverse graduated" remain eligible for IDA resources.

ECO-AUDIT
Environmental Benefits Statement

The World Bank Group is committed to reducing its environmental footprint. In support of this commitment, we leverage electronic publishing options and print-on-demand technology, which is located in regional hubs worldwide. Together, these initiatives enable print runs to be lowered and shipping distances decreased, resulting in reduced paper consumption, chemical use, greenhouse gas emissions, and waste.

We follow the recommended standards for paper use set by the Green Press Initiative. The majority of our books are printed on Forest Stewardship Council (FSC)-certified paper, with nearly all containing 50-100 percent recycled content. The recycled fiber in our book paper is either unbleached or bleached using totally chlorine-free (TCF), processed chlorine-free (PCF), or enhanced elemental chlorine-free (EECF) processes.

More information about the Bank's environmental philosophy can be found at http://www.worldbank.org/corporateresponsibility.